Lamps in the Darkness

By
ROY LAWSON TAWES

With an Introduction by
BISHOP EDWIN HOLT HUGHES

ABINGDON-COKESBURY PRESS
New York • Nashville

2565

Lamps in the Darkness

To My Parents
Good and Faithful
Who Kept a Guiding and Saving Light
In the Window of Home

Introduction

THE AUTHOR came to my distinct notice for the
first time when I read an open letter that he had written
to President Franklin D. Roosevelt. Our Chief Execu-
tive had made what I myself regarded as a rather pre-
carious request: that ministers of the gospel should
write him frankly their views of a mooted public question. I read a goodly number of the replies, but no one
of them impressed me as much as the communication
from this young pastor of the Eastern Shore. The
letter combined frankness with courtesy, strength with
kindness, conviction with breadth, while in its literary
form it was a model of English simplicity and force.
Sometime later, when a moral crusade was on in his
territory, he became the newspaper champion of the
right side and stepped forth to meet the Philistine
giants with effective sling and pebbles.

He has already given to the public one pleasing and
unique volume, *Laughing at the Saints*. Now comes
another, cast in a different form and dealing with a
figure of speech very commonly used in general literature and in the Holy Bible. It might seem difficult
to send light on light, but even a study of the outline
of this book will show that the author has done just
that. He has gathered radiance from the Sun of
Righteousness, and has poured it upon the words of
him who said that he was the Light of the World, and

that his followers were themselves to shine as lights in that world, holding forth the word of life.

The year in which this book comes from the press is a dark one. I am disposed to think that it is the darkest one in the world sense that I have ever known. Yet am I sure that this volume is a lantern, a lamp, an arc, a beacon, and that our people on the several continents will grope and grope, and stumble and stumble, until they find the Light that is presented in these pages.

EDWIN HOLT HUGHES

Foreword

WHEN THE night was dark on a lonely sea, my father would look for the beacon lights. He would sail his ship toward them and from them, thus setting a sure course that would bring him to the dawn. He knew where stood these lighted sentinels of the deep.

The pulpit in wartime must shine with certainty in a dark and lonely world. The preacher must know the spiritual truths for mankind in its blackout. He must be a permanent witness in a changing time, and bear his hopeful testimony to the Presence "who hath delivered us from the power of darkness." He need not hesitate to declare boldly the facts of Scripture and history.

The author of these sermons believes that our civilization is being shaken "that those things which cannot be shaken may remain." He does not despair of humanity. There are lights that have not gone out. *This is not the end of the world, but the end of an age that forgot God!*   R. L. T.

Acknowledgments

PERMISSION of authors and publishers to reprint selections quoted in this book is gratefully acknowledged, as follows:

Dodd, Mead and Company, Inc., for lines from "The House of Christmas" from *The Collected Poems of G. K. Chesterton*.

Ethel Romig Fuller for the poem "Proof."

Harcourt, Brace and Company for a selection from *Modern Man in Search of a Soul* by C. G. Jung.

Harper and Brothers for "I Have a Rendezvous With Life" by Countee Cullen.

Virgil Markham for lines from "Place of Peace" by Edwin Markham.

The Viking Press, Inc., for lines from "Coda" from *Not so Deep as a Well* by Dorothy Parker; copyright, 1926, 1928, 1931, 1936.

Alfred Grant Walton and Harper and Brothers, publisher, for lines from "Book of Books" from *Highways to Happiness*.

2565

Contents

11

I

THERE IS ALWAYS GOD

A Creed for the Crisis

WHEN DIED Richard Henry Harrison, gifted principal in the Negro cast of *Green Pastures*, the big daily published an arresting caption under his front-page photo. Words that stopped the reader were:

"DE LAWD" IS DEAD!

Our age has not been certain of God. Too much of modern life has been carelessly lived as if God did not exist any more. Now it is being said that man has nothing left to live for. When God goes, the purpose of living goes. Times of great darkness are upon us. The Christian faith must stand up to these times. Let us strike more the note of victory in our preaching. The pulpit should take the crepe off the door of heaven. We cannot afford to surrender the gospel to a world's despair. We ought not to exchange the lifelines of God for the headlines of man. Current events should not cause us to lose sight of the Good News. *God is not dead!* Let the militant church shout that mighty fact into the hearing of all human need. We are not without help. There is something that can be done about things as they are. We are not without hope. We can carry on until the morning, and in the morning we shall see the glory of the Lord.

Phillips Brooks, of the radiant pulpit, once told the students at Harvard: "Here is the last great certainty. Be sure of God, and in the end nothing can overthrow you." Little wonder that Helen Keller, triumphant over handicaps, upon first meeting with the noted preacher, spelled out the request of her soul: "Tell me, sir, what you know about God."

The essential message for troubled lives has the certainty of God in its content. The indispensable messenger for difficult situations is one who speaks positively with a "Thus saith the Lord." That messenger has the certainty of God possessed in his knowledge and experience. A fearful world of waning confidence and increasing darkness must have the message of light. It must have also the illumined messenger to make that message shine. The inner life can produce a working vocabulary and a saved personality. Men live at their very best in the pure strength of good words and good characters. It is up to the consecrated minds and yielded hearts of those who believe to make known their creed for the crisis. For those who will come to face soon the stern realities of being, and for those who are already at fighting grips with them, it is the holy assurance of a saving religion that there is always God.

God stands by. That blessed truth is a shining lamp in the darkness. It is a light that burns back into the centuries of history, and gleams toward fairer tomorrows. We can count on God. The prophet

Micah counted on God, and testified: *"When I sit in darkness, the Lord shall be a light unto me."* The prophet found One to help him see life through, and he lifted high his lamp for others. He promised his people that God's mercies would be renewed, that nations would be ashamed of their might, and that their sins would be cast into the depths of the sea.

Living Without God

Our worst folly has been to deify man. He makes a poor deity. We have talked the utter nonsense of his self-sufficiency. Man fails as a substitute for the Almighty. Progress fails as a substitute for redemption. The worship of man-made things is disastrous idolatry. Placing man at the center of the universe, and things at the center of his living, has had its tragic reaction in bitterest tears and deepest sorrows. The superman has come over the red horizon of modern war, marking his long and horrible trail of blood and flame. Humans are killed by the machines of their own making. A fool's paradise is under the destructive sword of judgment. Utopian plans for a new world order are smashed to bits. Boastful claims to an ever-advancing civilization are denied by global conflict. The "optimistic theology" of some pulpits is weighed in the balances, and found wanting. The permanent emancipation of man cannot be had in any temporary enslavement of his spirit. That spirit demands freedom in its recognition of God, and is creative only when building on firm foundations. A religion of humanity is not enough. We need a religion *for* humanity.

It is the present challenge and task of the church to recover its glorious gospel in the true worth of man. That worth is realized only in man's eternal importance and right relationship to God. Man cannot get along without his Maker. And God must be personal! Professor Einstein may not think so, but the combined evidence of human failure and guilt argues convincingly against his view. Man does need to know that God loves him, and that God is willing to forgive his sins. G. K. Chesterton declared:

> For men are homesick in their homes,
>   And strangers under the sun,
> And they lay their heads in a foreign land
>   Whenever the day is done.

God is not a voluntary absentee from modern life. He has been shown the door, and told plainly to get out. Life has dismissed him with a cruel indifference. That cruelty underlies man's inhumanity to man, and countless thousands mourn. God knows that we shall need him again, and that right early. That is the supreme reason for his staying near at hand.

God is not happy when his people weep.

God is not free when his prisoners are in concentration camps.

God is not without burdens when his refugees fill lonely roads from home.

God is not without pain when his multitudes suffer the agonies and heartaches of totalitarian strife.

16

There should be less complaint against God. Modern life has done too little service for him, and too much hurt to him. We are hardly in a position to blame him for our distress. The truth is—and we are being forced to its judgment—we are inwardly disturbed about pointing God to the exit. Outwardly we are too proud and stubborn to call him back. It is not an easy matter to admit failure, confess sin, humble self, and ask God for another chance. But that is the only way by which man arrives at his eternal worth. That is the way out we should be taking now. There is always God to make over human nature.

The drama *Street Scene* tells the story of life lived without God. Only once is the divine name mentioned, and that instance is a sarcastic implication of the divine character. Says the heroine of God: "I thought he was somebody who looked out for you and cared for you." That charge of the stage is serious. More serious still is the daily living of many people for whom God is an unconcerned nobody.

Living without God lends strong support to the world-wide movement of atheism. Living without God gives active approval to some dangerous and prevalent emphases on brute ancestry and animal behavior. Living without God denies the friendliness of the universe, the meaning of existence, and the hope of beyond.

Darkness has fallen over the several continents and the seven seas. Sin is having its awful fling. It has spread fears, brought griefs, locked chains, slain bodies, and ruined souls. Humanity afraid! Humanity cry-

17

ing! Humanity in bondage! Humanity staggering! Humanity broken! Humanity lost! Is there light anywhere? False prophets are quick to answer with their negatives of fate and resignations to doom. Why cannot religion as promptly answer with a helpful and harmonious chorus of affirmatives? We sometimes try to keep God in his other world, and out of this one. We look upon an evil environment, and are changed by it. We give up our spiritual heritage. Yet we are called to be saints in the household of Caesar. We are to be not conformed, but transformed. *O why do we forget that God came to dwell with us in Christ? O why do we forget that God bore a cross in his heart for the wrongs of a fallen world?*

God in the life of the world! There is that incalculable wealth for our spiritual poverty. His presence is our heaviest loss, and may be our richest gain. God is not eclipsed by the blackout any more than his stars are hid. With material values crashing, the kingdoms of men tottering, a whole civilization shaking, we may come into the immediate possession and power of this testimony: "When I sit in darkness, the Lord shall be a light unto me."

Good People Miss the Presence

There are good people that miss God. They have suffered pain, endured hardship, and struggled with doubt. Life has hit them with blinding blows. The church must distinguish, however, between pagan taunts and hearts of hunger. It must minister in love and patience and prayer to the disillusioned in its own membership. It is written victoriously into the records of Scripture that a doubting Thomas can become a worshiper with relit faith, and a wandering Cleopas tread a road of splendor. There is always God for those who sincerely seek him, and who will continue the search. Let us never put troubled saints in the same category with indifferent worldlings. The saints have overcome trial and tribulation, and discovered for themselves the meaning of Micah's word. Wrote Browning:

> So, let him wait God's instant men call years;
> Meantime hold hard by truth and his great soul,
> Do out the duty! Through such souls alone
> God stooping shows sufficient of his light
> For us i' the dark to rise by.

Saints of the Certainty

There is always God. That is the most meaningful certainty amid all the uncertainties. That is the most excellent certainty which we may have now in our grasp. That is the unfailing light "amid the encircling gloom." Henry P. Van Dusen has written of "human lives that make confidence in God inevitable." This is the magnificent calling of the saints. They do make it easier for others to believe in God. Said Sherlock Holmes to Dr. Watson: "You're the one fixed point in a world of change." What an applicable definition for sainthood! *Saints are fixed points in a changing world.* They know that God is, has been, and will be. He changes not. They know that

19

God has some eternal purpose for those whom he loves, and who love him. He will bring his purpose to pass. Toward that all creation moves. The saints have enough of personal trust to command in an emergency. To them life is much more than useless battle with hostile forces. There is always God. That spiritual defense makes for spiritual conquest.

Saints of the certainty defy the darkness. Dean Inge is far from "gloomy" when he sees the world as "a world for brave men." Redeemed boldness will alone drive back the sinful hordes of night. Weapons can destroy men, but not ideas. Life wins with God as an ally. He is more than they that are against us. To him who keeps the stars in space, bids the winter turn to spring, brings harvest from the seed, we can commit ourselves. Others have made that commitment, and God has not let them down. When it meant the bloody sweat of a Gethsemane, there came the strengthening angel. When it meant the piercing nails of a Calvary, there came resurrection morning with sunrise and lilies white. God is the last resort for times like these. Life needs to return unto him. Life needs to trust him all the way. Life needs to cling to the conviction that "all things work together for good to them that love God, *to them who are the called according to his purpose.*" God is able, and he will help us. He will give us wisdom for our foolishness. He will give us courage for our fear. He will line our clouds with precious promises. He will set his stars above the deathly shadows on our path.

Saints of the certainty have the light of God's reality. He is infinitely more than "a metaphor without significance to the modern mind." He is the final meaning of life for both modern minds and hearts. We may be conscious of his daily presence, and energized with his power. God is personal, available, and dependable. He loves his own, walks with them in the earth, and guides them through the pilgrimage. God is Creator, Ruler, Vindicator, and Saviour. He made this world, and it belongs to him. The foundations of the universe are laid in righteousness. There is the "one increasing purpose" of the ages. God hates sin, but for sinners his cross stands in the sky. Sainthood has a peculiar awareness of God's being around and within life. Sainthood has a sensitive conscience to the high callings of life in him. God is interested in human affairs, resident in human hearts, and expectant of human co-operation.

Saints of the certainty have the light of being right with God. They live in an understanding of the divine terms. They hold the world together. They have passion for the estranged soul of the individual. They have passion for the lost soul of society. There was great preaching done in the urgent invitation of an old evangelism: "Get right with God!" It was akin to the impassioned pleading of the apostle Paul: "We pray you in Christ's stead, be ye reconciled to God." Claims Dr. James Stewart that this problem of reconciliation is the crucial one of the hour. Man without God is restless of soul, and yet compelled by a sense of destiny. Soul rest and the reason for living are had in a new relationship established between the sinner forgiven and the forgiving God. Georgia Harkness reminds that we must find God in the monotones of life. Many feel now that sin has defeated every chance of the race. The different testimony of the saints ought to sound above the voices of desperation: "When I sit in darkness, the Lord shall be a light unto me." O let the redeemed of the Lord say so!

Saints of the certainty have the light of obligation to others. They attempt no selfish monopoly on God. They make good use of the darkness by lighting the steps of the pilgrimage for other feet. Religion loves and serves God while it is loving and serving man. The Social Gospel is no modern discovery. "God so loved the world." "If religion ends in self, it ends." A saved man wants others saved. In the commonplace talk of the postwar world the teachings of Jesus are more sentiment than experience. A new world cannot be builded on old sins. "Am I my brother's keeper?" is a question which we must face before God. Only as the saints rightly answer is there bright hope for the world.

Facing Facts

In a timely chapter by H. G. Wells a father and son discuss the fallen capitals of Europe. The son asks why such madness has been allowed to spread. The father wisely replies that the people have been too lazy or too blind or too preoccupied with little things to bother about the big things of life. *Indifference can be as fatal as unbelief.*

There is always God. Those who contend that religion will not face facts often ignore the fact of facts. Life refuses to act on the fact of God. Joseph Parker insisted: "If we seek to escape the reality of faith, we must submit to the reality of facts." The world facts are getting life down. While ignoring the necessity for a definite religious experience of God, men permit real and lasting values to slip through their fingers. We had better listen to the saints of certainty, and take them at their word. Science agrees that what has happened once may happen again. In every age the saints have experienced God.

Peace treaties do not prevent the distress of nations. Peace conferences do not insure the future. We are learning this lesson again at the sacrifice of our best youth. The ideal of democracy does not deter the mad dictators. Collapsed governments and conquered peoples, two world wars in one generation, indicate that something has gone wrong on the inside. *A blitzkrieg of military might is possible because sin first launched a successful blitzkrieg on personal character!* God has not been invited to sit at the peace tables! God has not had first place in the programs of national powers! Holy causes have been lost, and others are imperiled. Sacred traditions have been cast aside in rebellious attitudes toward the yesterdays. Men have proved themselves unworthy of good government, and disloyal to the precepts of righteousness. They have played politics and done business to the world's injury. There is always God. But life ignores him, and reckons not the judgments of history. God be prayed that we shall find the Light in this grim darkness, and be bet-

23

ter able for the job of another tomorrow! God speed the dawn!

Questionable legislation and economic scheming do not end depression. Prosperity cannot be had in sacrificing morals for revenue. Nor can it be had in the reckless spending of money. Even a "war boom" carries the threat of inflation. We may as well make up our minds that the kingdom of God is vitally related to the kingdoms of men. The eternal laws have not been repealed nor superseded. Jesus said: "My meat is to do the will of him that sent me." God's will—that is the first allegiance. Sin is man's chief problem, and its early solution is of vast import. Selfish appetite and gain, handouts and conflicts would not be headlines if an abiding sense of holy mission were written into the life lines of more souls. Our society is not a saved fellowship. There is always God. But life will not seek first his kingdom. Only in seeking and finding his kingdom is there the light of worth on human personality and brotherhood. "Man shall not live by bread alone."

Modern pleasures do not bring happiness. Too many amusements and pastimes are miserable escapes from reality. After the so-called fun and entertainment and thrills, people still have to live with themselves. There remains the prodigality of life, and the need for the Father's House. Happiness is not without, but within. Out of the heart are the issues of life. There is always God. But moderns ridicule the idea of joy in religion. Where else is light to shine in our night?

Science does not save us. The blessing can also

become the curse. Death rides in mechanized units. Bombs rain death from the sky. Torpedoes split a path of death through the sea. Bursting shell makes the city street a battlefield of death. Gases hold whole populations in terror of death. There is always God. But we have not had the Spirit in the wheels of a machine age. Plenty of light at the touch of a button, but blackout curtains on the windows! We have willfully destroyed connections with the Power from above.

Education should be penitent. We have not sent out from our schools the character to control intelligence. We have gone haywire in our teaching. Just two years ago a prominent educator pleaded for doing away with Christian morals. Said he: "Cruelty, selfishness, lust, cowardice, and deceit are normal ingredients of human nature which have their useful role in the struggle for existence. Intrinsically they are all virtues." All teaching, to be sure, has not been so extreme. Too little of it, however, has taken in God. We have educated for efficiency, and not emergency. We have thought of success, and not failure. We have determined to get things, and forgot that things could get us. We have debated the roots of war, and not met the conditions of peace. We have graded the scholarship of mind, and made no allowance for the loyalties of heart. There is always God. But deaf ears have been turned to the teachings of the Bible, the Holy Son, and the church. The most brilliant light shines in God's written, living, and experienced word.

Religion must be more than profession. There is

lacking a practical faith in God. Mouthings about
God are not testimonies of spiritual rebirth. We do not
hesitate to condemn the dictatorships. Listen! Will
the democracies dare to stand up before God, and declare themselves Christian in conduct? God pity us,
and forgive us; WE HAVE ALL SINNED! There is always
God. But we have not taken him seriously enough to
entrust life to his hands. We have not chosen to
walk in the light as he is in the light.

The Return to God

Joseph Conrad exclaimed: "Give me the right word,
and the right accent, and I will move the world!" *The
right word is God. The right accent is man redeemed in the Christ of God.*

America's need, the world's need, is a revival of religion—a revival like unto those stirrings of soul in
past periods that changed history. This generation
has never witnessed a real revival. O let us pray for
an outpouring of spiritual power upon the people!
"Wilt thou not revive us again: that thy people may rejoice in thee?" God has ready an answer to that
prayer. "If my people, which are called by my name,
shall humble themselves, and pray, and seek my face,
and turn from their wicked ways; then will I hear from
heaven, and will forgive their sin, and will heal their
land." What a blessing of light for times of darkness!

Keepers of the Faith

We need more than a revival of religion. We must
keep the faith after the revival comes. Present de-

liverance should promise future security. When God comes into life, he comes to stay. When God abides, life stands for something good and beautiful and true. The world becomes a larger setting for the new man and his mission. Humanity benefits from character in service.

There is always God. We are not always Christian. Instead of going forward, we backslide. We let revival fires die on the altar, and our hearts grow cold. We cease loving men, and again hatred finds expression. We do not undergird peace, and war breaks out. We condone sin, and the tempter grabs opportunity. We empty church pews, and life is left with a vacancy. We are indifferent to spiritual matters, and "things are in the saddle and ride mankind."

The prophet Micah chose to keep his faith. We can make no wiser choice. The prophet relied on spiritual resources. We may have them. The man of God endured as seeing him who is invisible. That is the tried and tested secret of human endurance. That is the experience of the victor. "When I sit in darkness, the Lord shall be a light unto me."

> . . . . If I stoop
> Into a dark tremendous sea of cloud,
> It is but for a time; I press God's lamp
> Close to my breast; its splendor, soon or late,
> Will pierce the gloom: I shall emerge one day.

II

JESUS SAVES

Light on the Future

PROPHET ISAIAH saw the future's great light of the Incarnation brilliant over seven centuries. A present crisis did not destroy his vision nor silence his voice. His message looked ahead to better days for his people. Even now they could have the inspiration and power of a new confidence and a new promise. *"They that dwell in the land of the shadow of death, upon them hath the light shined."*

Sang the angels when, in the fullness of time, Messiah came to deliver his people from their distresses. Worshiped wise men and humble shepherds when the Saviour came to save his people from their sins. Shone the Star of Bethlehem when Herod's ugly shadow fell across the path of pilgrims of the soul.

The Lord Jesus Christ is the world's Messiah and Saviour! He is at once the perfect revelation of God to man, and the perfect hope of man in God. The prophetic vision was of no small Christ. The prophetic voice spoke not of a manly Galilean. One should come big enough for all human need. Some modern effort would reduce Jesus. It would give us only his humanity. Surely we would not part with that. But we do not have him enough in having him as the best of humans. We must have him as God in the flesh.

Jesus does not save as a man. Yet there was in his manhood no fault at all. His worst enemies could not pick a flaw in his character. His closest friends marveled at his living. Multitudes felt the impact of his presence. Earth has never known human perfection comparable to his walk among men.

Jesus does not save as a teacher. Yet in his teachings there were lessons of life beyond the texts of all schools. The wisest were impressed by his strange wisdom. His words carried the sound of authority. No other teacher has had his teachings so vindicated by the events of time.

Jesus does not save as a reformer. Yet in his original emphasis on the sacredness of personality there was incentive for better living. So original was his earthly approach to individual and social righteousness that he divided history between B.C. and A.D.

Jesus does not save as a martyr. Yet in his death there was an unyielding allegiance to a holy cause. There was also a different departure at Calvary. One cross has stood above all other crosses on the skyline of life.

Jesus saves only as the Redeemer. His manhood was perfect, his teachings were without error, his crusades had eternity in them, his death was distinctive, because of his unique sonship with the Father. Those who reject the redemptive ministry of Jesus ignore his own testimony and witness to his person

and works. O my soul! believe that he was Deity
here with life.

> Let all my words and actions be
> A testimony, Lord, for thee,
> And thy redeeming love.

Jesus saves. That is a shining lamp in the darkness.
Let the pulpit hold it up. Let the people see it.
Light for a warring, sinning, suffering, dying, lost
world! Light on the future!

A Change in the Program

There was a change of program on the radio. A
news bulletin interrupted the regular broadcast to tell
more of war's horror. Then the broadcast was re-
sumed with a chorus singing: "All hail the power of
Jesus' name! . . . . And crown Him Lord of all." Dare
we believe that there can be such a decisive change in
the world's program of life? Jesus can effect that
change by being acknowledged Lord in the lives of
men.

Let Jesus reign over our pulpits. Says James Reid:
"Real preaching is the redemptive agony of a real man,
bringing to the needs of men a knowledge of the only
true God in Jesus Christ." That commentary is one
of rigid self-examination, but only the preaching of
the Bible can minister effectively to this age. Trifling
with minor themes brings judgment upon our calling.
The Bible is not discredited, but neglected. People
need to know more about it. The day of the parson
may have passed, because the pew is well informed

today on many subjects. But the day of the preacher
is here, because the pew is not wise in the things of
Scripture. God's supreme revelation in Jesus Christ is
the preacher's major theme. With a world on fire, and
humanity in the flames, let him preach the saving presence of the Son of God.

Let Jesus reign over our pews. Speaks Arthur Gos-
sip of the early Christians: "They come bursting in
with their faces shining and their hearts afire, crying
out, 'We have got it, we have got it!—the thing tired
earth has been waiting for. We have got it, and we
must share it with the world!'" O wondrous marks
of the gift of salvation! *Faces shining! Hearts afire!
Sharing life!* Religion is not long-faced, freezingly
cold, self first. In these times of bleeding hearts some
religious literature is circulated that does grave injustice to the Christ. He had the face that children
loved. He had the heart that loved all people. He
gave himself wholly to others. For the joy that was
set before him, he endured the cross. For the sins of
mankind he prayed forgiveness. And he died that
others might live the abundant life.

The Fact of Sin

Jesus saves from sin. The light of the gospel shines
upon the land of the shadow of death. It is light from
the love of God for the lost. Sin is the most terrible
and deadly fact in human experience. We are not re-
sisting it as we should. Some reactions of the modern
mind have tried to explain sin away. Many experts
would remove the word from the vocabulary of reli-

31

gious speech. The word is already tabooed in certain social and educational circles. Meanwhile the talkies and best sellers, news sheets and radios, present sin as a fact in today's life.

Sin is not a stumble upward when the Bible looks upon man fallen in his iniquity.

Sin is more than an error when the Bible views it as a willful act of eternal consequence.

Sin is not a blundering quest for God when the Bible warns of the sure road to ruin and dead end.

The world's lostness and confusion is the work of sin and sinners. If we so choose, we may see the tragedy of our times through rose-colored glasses. We may congratulate ourselves that man uses his science for mass destruction in the sky and on land and sea. We may seek to justify man's using his powers to crush his fellow men. We may even soft-pedal the lusts of the flesh that give origin to wars and moral collapse. *But an artificial optimism is as fatal as a fascinating pessimism.* We need to see things as they are with the stark realism of Jesus. We need a Saviour's-eye view of the world. Man is fallen to lowest depths of sin, and the Christ of the cross can lift him to higher ground.

The story is told of an illiterate woman and the visit of a circuit-rider among the mountaineers. He preached the gospel of Calvary at a family gathering. When he had finished his message, this illiterate woman, speaking for the group, questioned: "Stranger, when did you say all this yere happened?" "A long time ago," was the reply—"nearly two thousand years ago." "And they nailed him to that thar tree when he hadn't done nothin' to hurt them—only jist loved them?" Then, with a broken shout and sobbing voice, "Wal, stranger, let's hope it ain't so!"

It is so that sin meant the cross. The continued rejection of that truth reveals the awfulness of man's guilt. Christ is crucified afresh. Sometimes the human attitude is very harsh, as reflected in a bit of modern verse from a college sheet:

> I fight alone and win or sink,
>   I need no one to make me free;
> I want no Jesus Christ to think
>   That he could die for me.

The Gift of Salvation

Jesus saves to eternal life. Here is more light for the darkness. We must not let this lamp go out, but keep it burning in our hearts. It is the wonderful promise of the Forever amid time's change and decay. It is the joyful New Life amid the wandering old life of wicked ways. It is Faith's security amid the crash of material values. It is Love's blessings amid the hatreds of the race. Forgiveness of sin lifts man into an experience of One who abides with, lives in, and keeps the saved unto the uttermost.

Man must confess that he is a sinner to know the freedom of a full pardon. Man cannot forgive himself. He has tried that, and been disturbed in conscience still. He must look unto the Saviour. Man cannot obtain salvation in his own name. He has tried that, and found his works alone to be without merit.

33

In the name of Jesus he must come to the altar of repentance. Man cannot be saved by reference to good heredity or environment. He has tried that, and has had to face his own responsibility and failure. In complete surrender of all that he is, and can possibly be, he must pledge himself in service to his Lord.

Salvation is the gift of God in eternal life through Jesus Christ. To appropriate the gift there must be a recognized need for divine forgiveness. Many moderns would not be a responsive audience to a Jonathan Edwards preaching of "sinners in the hands of an angry God." But there is too little concern about God's being in the hands of apathetic sinners. It would be the occasion of spiritual blessing and power and triumph if we sought more the possession of eternal life. We foolishly essay to live one world at a time. Man cannot succeed at that. Time and eternity are together in his life.

Eternal life may be ours now. There is more than the idea of continuity in it. There is *quality*. We may rejoice in the salvation of him who "delivered us from so great a death, and doth deliver: in whom we trust that he will yet deliver us." "This is life eternal, that they might know thee the only true God, and Jesus Christ, whom thou hast sent." To be sure, we need a stronger faith in personal immortality. We need also an overflowing experience of eternal life which has beginning now. The Christian's road ends in heaven, the city of God. The Christian's road starts here in the country of man. Life is already saved and already new when lived in the saving presence of Christ. Quality is a familiar word. It ought to characterize a familiar life. If salvation has any meaning at all, it is in the purpose we give to our lives in the earth. Life is not worth going on here-after if it is not worth going on here. "They that dwell in the land of the shadow of death, upon them hath the light shined."

> We would see Jesus! We would look upon
> The light in that divinely human face,
> Where lofty majesty and tender grace
> In blended beauty shone.
>
> We would see Jesus, and let him impart
> The truth he came among us to reveal,
> Till in the gracious message we should feel
> The beating of God's heart.

Gleams From Calvary

An artist painted the portrait of Alexander the Great so as to hide the scars on the general's forehead. The artists of Scripture do not attempt to hide the scars of Jesus. They identify him by them. As W. E. Sangster aptly suggests, there is a pledge in those glorious scars. The great light from above is upon them.

Jesus saves to an abiding faith in the love of God. It has not been easy to believe in that love amid "the maddening maze of things." People have lived under pressure. Neither was the cross easy for God. God loved enough to give his best. The cross reveals the eternal passion for a panting planet. Love is the one grand explanation of Calvary. We do not under-stand it all, but we do know that love was there.

35

Love gave all to redeem man. The Heavenly Father sacrificed supremely for earth's family. In that immeasurable act was sufficient proof of his love for all mankind. Hear the saintly G. H. Morrison pray: "Lord, I have reasoned with thee. I have marshalled all my arguments and all my facts, and I am here to confess that by the fact of Calvary thou hast won." O the love of God toward us! Suffering, sacrificial, self-giving love! Sin-hurt, sin-atoning, burden-bearing love! Love, pardoning the world's guilt! Love, dying to save! Love of God for his creation!

Jesus saves to a conviction of sin's seriousness. If sin cost God a heartbreak, we cannot afford to be at heart's ease. If once we see sin in the light that breaks through Calvary's darkness, we will take time out for decision and action. It is always good evidence to salvation to be at prayer and labor for the lost. The sense of lostness must be kept alive in the life of man. With sin striking terror at the hearts of nations, corrupting society, destroying personalities, the Christian must put on the whole armor of God to fight the devil. Walter Lippmann in one of his columns admitted that our fathers had something in their thought of "satanic majesty." The world's wickedness is real, and the tragic results are seen. Let the church preach God's intense hatred of sin, and his eternal love for sinners. Let the church witness to its gospel in a happy experience of its own salvation. Just as first-century Christianity refused to worship the emperor, so must today's church be the church in a pagan environment. Judgment is upon the world.

Let judgment begin with us, O church of Christ! Wherein have we sinned, and come short of the glory of God? Wherein have we compromised our position, surrendered our ideals, lost our distinctions?

Jesus saves to a certain triumph over the things of this world. Christians are overcomers. *The "V" in Calvary is for victory!* We are more than conquerors in Christ. There is excess victory. Christians get the Upper Hand on life. They meet opposition with the Unfailing Helper. They companion with the Faithful Friend. They follow the Unerring Guide. They listen to the Voice of Authority. They win with the Power not their own. They march in confidence, live in love, are led under inspiration, have daily assurance of the divine presence, and are victors under the Captain of their salvation.

There is an old negro spiritual with the repeated questioning: "Were you there when they crucified my Lord?" The triumphant life answers Yes. Dr. F. B. Meyer's testimony is timely for our lips: "I am not going to die for my sins. I did that nineteen hundred years ago." The soldiers of the cross can drive sin into retreat. The victory belongs to Christ, and therefore to them. The world gave Jesus a cross of shame, and he handed it back the cross of honor. Life did its very worst to him, and he returned to life his very best. Men thought that they had ended him, but he brought men to a new beginning. Sin plunged creation into darkness, but the cross was lighted with the Light of the World.

Jesus saves to the blessed hope of his coming and

crowning. In one of Masefield's plays a centurion tells Pilate's wife that Christ will not be stopped. The world will not hold back the destined reign of our Lord. We have no defeated Saviour. We have reason to continue praying: "Thy kingdom come." That prayer will be answered. Even those who pierced him shall look upon him again. God marches on in Christ! The early Christians had as their watchword *"Maranatha!"*—"O Lord, come!" That watchword did make a difference in their living. Some may ask: "Where is the promise of his coming?" Things seem as they were. This note of frustration is added to the sad music of humanity in a strange land. We have still the blessed hope, and it will be realized. The same prophet of the text, who saw the future's great light in Christ, said also concerning him: *"He shall not fail."*

Some thought that after Calvary Jesus had failed. They could not see the Bright and Morning Star. They could not hear the rustle of angels' wings. They knew the seal of empire was on his tomb. Even the doors of the Upper Room were shut for fear. BUT EASTER CAME, AND PENTECOST. And with them Christ came again. He lives, and the future is his. We who are his have a part in the coming kingdom. There is light in the land of the shadow of death. The angels are nigh. The seal of empire will be broken. The morning of resurrection and the day of revival will come.

When the mechanized units of Germany advance no more, when the Roman eagles have folded their wings in peace, when the Russian bear has been chained, when the Alps no longer know the tramp of marching armies, when tears are dried in the eyes of neutrals who did not want to fight, when Bethlehem's Star of the East floods with radiance the Near and Far East, when new Simons lift up the cross in Africa, when the British lion has ceased his growling, when the last stain of sin is gone from the stars and stripes of Old Glory—*there will be Jesus.*

Jesus saves! Now! Forever!

III

THE COMFORTER IS HERE

The Best Recommendation

THE COMING of Dwight L. Moody to a certain city was being discussed by a group of representative churchmen. The several successes of the famed evangelist were brought to the attention of those present. One unimpressed member asked, "Does Mr. Moody have a monopoly of the Holy Ghost?" To which another replied with conviction, "No, but the Holy Ghost has a monopoly of Mr. Moody." There could not have been a better recommendation for God's good man. The evangelist came to that city, and the Holy Ghost came with him in a manifestation of revival power.

The best possible recommendation for this troubled age would be to have the Holy Ghost fill it with power and zeal for righteousness.

The Comforter is here to lighten the world's darkness. He would console in sorrow, encourage in fear, guide over rough places, and impart the strength for journeying. He would bring order from chaos, inspire men and reveal the truth, witness to the salvation of Christ and the presence of God, and enable the church to preach to the ingathering of souls.

40

THE COMFORTER IS HERE

A Neglected Doctrine

The doctrine of the Holy Ghost is neglected in today's pulpit and pew. Although we live in his dispensation, we are indifferent to this third person of the Trinity. We contend that the doctrine is beyond explanation. We boast that we are done with superstition. We will have no fear in the experience of religion. We insist that changing the word "Ghost" to "Spirit" does not help us to think in terms of personality.

It is not very complimentary to the modern mind to reject that which it cannot explain. Henry Drummond's words have not lost their timeliness: "Life still wanders through science without a definition, yet we do not deny that there is life."

Moderns are not rid of superstition. They anxiously await messages from their dead through human mediums. They have their fortunes told through the readings of human palms. They seek to avoid unlucky days and numbers.

The times are not free from fear, but afflicted with fears. Ministers now pursue special studies in psychiatry. Doctors consult with religionists, and even advise attendance at church. Religion is related to human ailments. We seem to be just catching up with Jesus on that. Nervous breakdowns, mental disorders, suicides, discouragements, discords, defeats—all bear pitiable testimony to the fact that people are afraid.

Men deny the personal God despite the evidence of creation, the characters of the Bible, the assurances of Jesus, the witnessing of the early church, and the

41

experience of present-day saints. Men deny the Saviour of persons, although the fact of personal salvation is historic. Men deny personality to the Holy Spirit because his workings are invisible.

The Comforter is here. We may have this shining lamp in the darkness. The Holy Spirit speaks God's call to life. The Holy Spirit is sent to "convict the world in respect of sin, and of righteousness, and of judgment." The Holy Spirit can make real the redemptive gift of Christ. The Holy Spirit can fill believers with power.

Cried the psalmist of old: "*Whither shall I go from thy spirit? . . . . If I say, Surely the darkness shall cover me; even the night shall be light about me.*" O let us recover this precious doctrine of the Holy Spirit, and have comfort and help on life's way.

What the Bible Says

The Bible is emphatic in teaching the personality of the Holy Spirit. This Personality is everywhere, and reveals both God and Christ in nearness to our needs. The Bible teaches the deity of the Holy Spirit with divine names, divine attributes, and divine works. He is presented as the Active Agent in creation, the saving witness to Christ in reproof of the world, and a realized Presence in the experience of the Christian. He is the Author of Scripture, the Inspirer of men, the Illuminator of the soul. He equips and assures the believer. He revives and empowers the church.

The teachings of the Bible have survived all the attacks of time, and the church has outlived all its opposition of the past. The personality of the Holy Spirit is in the creed of confession and the apostolic benediction. In the formula of baptism, the ceremony of marriage, and the committal of the dead we acknowledge the living presence of the Holy Spirit. In sustaining beliefs and bestowed blessings, at the beginning and ending of this earthly life, in the holiness of love, the Comforter is here.

What Christ Says

In that masterpiece chapter of John fourteen, Christ promises his disciples: "The Comforter, which is the Holy Ghost, whom the Father will send in my name, he shall teach you all things, and bring all things to your remembrance, whatsoever I have said unto you."

All things!

All things pertaining to the kingdom of God!

All things related to man's eternal welfare!

The Holy Spirit teaches not the things of the world's wisdom. He instructs in the lessons of God. He testifies of Christ. He upholds the divine purpose. He unfolds the glory of divine love. He persuades to a saving faith. He makes plainer the way of redemption. He clothes the words of the Redeemer with all authority. He establishes the Christian in righteousness, anoints him for service, and gives him heirship to eternal life.

We are not alone. We are not left comfortless. Wherever we are, and however we are, God is accessible. The night need not cover us. The Comforter will make it light about us. J. H. Jowett preached: "We may know that we have him by our glowing love, by our redeeming helpfulness, by our continual charity, by our indestructible patience." We are to love God and man. We are saved to serve, and we serve to save. We must sacrifice in sharing with others. We must wait on the Lord, and allow him time enough to work.

In the wonderful and precious promise of Christ, the Holy Spirit is the Sent One: it has not been long since our fathers and mothers sang prayerfully:

> O Lord, send the power just now,
> And baptize everyone!

The individual, the nation, the world need such a fresh baptism of spiritual power. The Greek word for power, *dynamis*, is our word "dynamite." Baptized of the Holy Ghost, life comes into possession of great power. There was enough dynamite at Pentecost to blow up an empire, and blast thrones to dust.

The scholarly T. R. Glover thinks that the history of Christianity gathers around four men: Paul, Augustine, Luther, and Wesley. What dynamite! Yet they had not the power until life was "all out" in consecration and separation. Then, the fellowship of the cross and the power of the resurrection. Then, the experience of personal devotion and intimate communion. Then, the service of salvation by faith. Then, the happy results of revival.

In the wonderful and precious promise of Christ, the Holy Spirit brings the Master's words to remembrance. Hear this invitation of the Christ: "If any man thirst, let him come unto me, and drink." There must be a consuming thirst for God. There must be an overwhelming want of the Saviour. Man is privileged to drink of the Fountain that never runs dry. No one drink satisfies. There must be daily drinkings for a Spirit-filled life. Growth in grace is not automatic. It is essential that we drink of the Living Water, and we ourselves become wells of water springing up into everlasting life.

It is said that a student in old Professor Duncan's class quoted: "I know in whom I have believed." "Repeat that passage," requested the kindly teacher. The passage was repeated as at the first. Then the student was counseled: "My dear sir, you must never let even a preposition come between you and your Saviour!" Nothing between! The Holy Spirit will keep clear the right of way.

A Ministry That Helps

The Comforter is here to minister unto a suffering people. He would have us enter into the help of "a garland for ashes, the oil of joy for mourning, the garment of praise for the spirit of heaviness." All things work together for good to the lovers and called of the Lord. The night shall not cover us. There is light about us.

Let one more attest,
I have lived, seen God's hand through a lifetime, and all was
for best.

Even as the Son of God suffered, so must we suffer in the wise Providence over life and the purposes of

45

the Heavenly Father. We can none claim exemption from the common lot. If we are brought through suffering to a more intimate fellowship with God, if the disciplines of life make stronger faith and awaken hope, if pain rekindles a flame in the night, if our own crosses make us more deeply conscious of Calvary, if the virtues of our peace and patience influence others to holy living, we shall indeed be successful in a ministry that helps.

Margaret Barrie's intended husband, a young preacher, was killed in an accident. She had her distinguished brother, Sir James, write to the members of the saddened parish: "My sister is not afraid. God, who gave his Son for the redemption of the world, has told her that he had need of this disciple's life. So God chose his own way and took her Jim, her dear young minister. And she says 'God's will be done,' and she thanks him for taking away so suddenly only one who was ready to face his Maker without a moment's notice. And she says that you are not to grieve for her overmuch, *for she is in God's keeping*." "The night shall be light about me."

> Come, ye disconsolate, where'er ye languish,
>   Come to the mercy seat, fervently kneel;
> Here bring your wounded hearts, here tell your anguish:
>   Earth has no sorrow that heaven cannot heal.

Divine Company for Lonely Lives

The Comforter is here, because life cannot go on alone. The New Testament benediction of the apostle is for lonely lives: "The communion of the Holy Spirit be with you all." There is more than a blessing pronounced in this exultant benediction. There is prevailing prayer in it. Paul desires earnestly the better gifts for his people. He wants them to stand up to life. He knows the courage necessary for that position. So he prays. He knows the mighty fortress of his God. He is sure that the Captain of his salvation goes forward to victory. He senses the need for good soldiers of Jesus Christ. He is unyielding in his conviction that life's battle belongs unto the Lord.

We are not alone. We have divine company for lonely lives. Thank God for that meaningful fact written so largely and impressively into the life of the Christian. The Comforter abides. Minds are freed from troublous doubts, and saved from fatal unbelief. Hearts are healed of aching hurts, and filled with wondrous love. Souls are delivered from sin, and made to rejoice in abundant pardon. Lives are lifted from depths of trial to heights of faith. Losses are transformed into invaluable gains. Defeats are turned to lustrous triumphs. Prayers are heard and answered, and we rise conquerors from our knees. Our service counts from the cup of cold water pressed to thirsty lips to the soul won in the gospel. And death finds us unafraid with our hope of the world to come.

Life is victorious in the constant help and daily presence of the Holy Spirit. Life gives up its prodigality for God the Father. Life wins over the tempter with God the Son. We cannot fall with the Everlasting

Arms beneath us. We cannot turn back with the Eternal Voice speaking its forgiveness and cheer and promise. We are loved and understood and redeemed. The Comforter is here to make night light about us.

The Spirit and the Life

The called life expresses the Spirit. There is personal witnessing. There is holy behavior. The coming of the Holy Ghost was necessary to the birth of the church. Without that power the church cannot live. The indwelling of the Holy Ghost was the compulsion of early disciples in their tasks as Christian evangelists. We are powerless without that presence. The Bible states: "The fruit of the Spirit is love, joy, peace, longsuffering, gentleness, goodness, faith, meekness, temperance." It has been suggested that a colon might be placed after love. All the other graces spring from that. Fruit is singular, and the Christian's life is a united whole.

Samuel Wesley once penned these words to his son Charles: "Charles, be steady. The Christian faith will surely revive in these kingdoms. You shall see it, though I shall not." The Holy Spirit broke the darkness over England, and the sins of a people were burnt out with revival fire.

O come to us, Holy Spirit! Let not the darkness cover us!

> Come as the light: to us reveal
> Our sinfulness and woe;
> And lead us in those paths of life
> Where all the righteous go.

IV

THE BIBLE HAS NOT BEEN DESTROYED

"The Word of the Lord Endureth For Ever"

THE BIBLE is not a book-of-the-month. The Bible is the Book-of-the-Ages. It replaces the fiction of man with the fact of God. It sets over against the popular writings of these times the timeless writings of those moved by the Holy Ghost. The Bible is the unread best seller for modern readers. The Bible is the neglected book without which no one is up with his reading. The Bible is the principal book in the home, but it is not enough in the home life. The Bible is the greatest book in the nation, but knowledge of its message is lacking among both leaders and citizenry. The Bible is the most precious volume of life, but men are indifferent to the possession of it.

The Bread of Life has not been rationed. The Bible is an open book for all the people. Whosoever will may come to know the bountiful feast of its inspired pages.

Here is not the bold wisdom of a bragging world. Here are saving doctrines for fallen man.

Here is not the sour sneer of cynicism. Here is the strong condemnation of all wrong, and triumph of the best.

Here is not unhindered self-expression. Here is voluntary self-restraint.

Here is not racy entertainment for curious eyes and filthy minds. Here is sound instruction for unlearned and unredeemed hearts.

The Bible endures. No other book has its Author. No other book has its theme. No other book has its message to men. No other book has its authority and inspiration. No other book offers its solutions to human problems, and its answers to life's questions. No other book rings with such certainty. No other book so estimates personal worth. No other book so mends broken relationships. No other book so encourages faith, enlivens hope, and sweetens love. No other book so reveals the value of time, the trust of life, and the reward of eternity. The Bible is a shining lamp in the darkness. Said the psalmist: *"Thy word is a lamp unto my feet, and a light unto my path."*

"The Entrance of Thy Words Giveth Light"

The Bible has one main road for getting home to God. There are rough places in it. There are steep hills to climb. There are thorns and briars that prick. There are deep waters to cross. But as man goes on and through, he builds his altars of worship. He knows God the Lover, Jesus Christ the Saviour, the Holy Spirit as Guide.

The main road of the Bible leads from Eden lost to Paradise regained. From the fall of human nature to redeemed man in risen glory. From the Garden where sin came to the Garden where sin can never come. From the flaming sword of judgment to the open gates of welcome. From wasted opportunities of life to eternal service for the King of kings. From forsaken love to First Love's return. From darkest night to brightest morning. From time's little while to eternity's forever. From sad farewells to glad greetings. From pain to healing. From loss of loved ones to reunion of hearts. From heavy crosses to the crowns of overcomers.

> How precious is the book divine,
> By inspiration given!
> Bright as a lamp its doctrines shine,
> To guide our souls to heaven.

"Through Thy Precepts I Get Understanding"

The Bible is a lamp and a light for our thoughts about the universe. It shines with the presence of the Creator, who alone could say: "Let there be light." There is no better explanation for the origin of things than that offered in the verses of Genesis. We see there the God of creation. We see that planets do not spin in space by chance. We see that man is not a cosmic accident. The Bible claims with truth: "In the beginning God created. . . . ." The Bible also announces the persistent purpose of creation: "God saw that it was *good*." And God has not left the universe to run itself. It runs according to his law, and on his schedule. There is a divine reason why seasons come and go, tides rise and fall, day and night alternate, seedtime brings harvest. God has not left his people of the universe the playthings of fate. His purpose still holds its onward course. God has us in his mind and heart. Knowing the stars by name, watching the sparrow's fall, seeing the flowers bloom, numbering the sands, commenting on the grasses, he gives to man the pre-eminence in creation. Of supremest import in the universe is the reconciliation of that child to the Father.

Man is the workmanship of God. Although he be a prodigal of the far country, there burns a lamp in the window of the Father's House. The light falls on the way home. There is ever satisfaction for the homesickness of the soul. The Bible is alone in its light on the worth of man, and its conception of human personality. Eternity is set in the hearts of earth's pilgrims and strangers. Sometimes a man is lost amid the bigness of his surroundings and the facts of his experiences. He hears a Bertrand Russell predict: "All the labors of the ages, all the devotion, all the inspiration, all the noonday brightness of human genius are destined to extinction in the vast death of the solar system, and the whole temple of man's achievement must inevitably be buried beneath the debris of a universe in ruins." Still the Bible champions the cause of man. It marks his being as of holy origin, calls him to a holy mission, and points him to a holy destination. It blows the wind of dignity, and refreshes the atmosphere of despair. It rains the rain of faith, and settles the dust of materialism. It shines the warmth of character, and burns the rubbish of license. O man! the Bible urges to a goal, challenges to a task, invites to success, cheers to victory, exalts goodness, and glorifies life.

The Bible is a lamp and a light penetrating the darkness of these times. The Bible presents life as the gift of God. It erects the cross to redeem life. It records the resurrection to give life power over sin and death. It tells of Pentecost to stir life to the ministry of evangelism. It opens the gates of the temple for life's worship. There are voices that cry out against life. Only yesterday Disraeli pronounced "youth a blunder, manhood a struggle, and old age a regret." Many would agree with him. Today a Dreiser calls life "a complete illusion which changes and eludes one at every point." Many feel that way about it. The Bible asks youth to remember God, manhood to be strong and brave, and age to be hopeful. The Bible offers to all the abundant life as lived by Christ, and in him.

The Bible has not been destroyed. We have its choice treasures of truth about the universe and man and life—the creative expressions of God's love and will—

> That God, which ever lives and loves,
> One God, one law, one element,
> And one far-off divine event,
> To which the whole creation moves.

"Teach Me Thy Way, O Lord"

The Bible is a lamp and a light for the mind of youth. John Ruskin was unashamed of a good mother who read her Bible. Said the son in tribute: "This maternal instillation of my mind in that property of chapters I count very confidently the most precious, and on the whole, the one essential part of my education." Others with Ruskin bear eloquent testimony to the influence of a mother's Bible.

The work of religious education needs to be begun early. An undying memory of the Christian home is that regular reading of the Bible in family devotions. A lasting impression of Godly parentage is that simple interpretation of Scripture by those who looked into the souls of their children. *Too much religious education has not been religious.* One who has taught at camp and institute and training school knows about the appalling Biblical ignorance of young people from good homes and prominent churches. The young people are "more to be pitied than censured." We must be honest enough to take the blame as parents and teachers. We have not made proper use of our Bibles. Children grow up in a world that uses every means to educate them falsely. We cannot meet such a serious situation by being afraid of what the Bible says, nor by freeing religion from restrictions. Youth needs something more than a denial of the supernatural, a legendary tale, a nature story, hero worship, or a life's calling without individual regeneration. Youth is not challenged by our apologies for the faith and emphasis on an easy conscience. Youth wants something to believe in and live for. Give youth that, and youth will fall in line. We ought to know this truth from the national movements across the sea. But we want youth for the cross and not the swastika. "Wherewithal shall a young man cleanse his way? by taking heed thereto according to thy word." "And that from a child thou hast known the holy scriptures, which are able to make thee wise unto salvation through faith which is in Christ Jesus."

Huxley was an agnostic, but he defended the reading of the Bible in public school. He knew the history of England, and the nation's obligation to the Bible. He called the Bible "the Magna Charta of the poor and of the oppressed, the most democratic book in all the world." We allow the Bible to be kept out of the public school. *We permit modern education to exile God.* Let us be mindful of our national history and heritage. Remember that the Bible built "the little red schoolhouse on the hill," and raised the flag above it. It is argued that there must be academic freedom. Must there be chains on the word of God? Must we continue to employ teachers whose minds run riot, and not resist their affronts to the sanctities of life? Must we stand by and see lesser literature and inferior morals praised, and this masterpiece of noblest literature and highest morals scorned? Are our youth to swallow the poison of fatalistic philosophies, and be denied an infilling of the only sensible, workable philosophy by which to live?

I believe in the separation of church and state. I believe that the classroom is not a place for sectarian pressure. But I also believe that EDUCATION NEEDS A SENSE OF GOD! The founding fathers did not intend that he should be kept out. A widely known educator declares that fully eighty per cent of our youth are unprepared by the schools to take up the duties of life. A daily reading and helpful presentation of the Bible would aid in preparation and direction for life's work. Wise men of old knew how to live, what to do, and where to go. They learned and taught from a knowledge and experience grounded deeply in the truth of the Bible. And it is written of the Great Teacher: "Then opened he their understanding, that they might understand the scriptures." Because we have not sat at the feet of Jesus, civilization needs to be more civilized.

"Righteousness Exalteth a Nation"

The Bible is a lamp and a light for the nation. William Tyndale, translator of the Bible, was strangled and burned at the stake. Before death came he prayed: "O Lord, open thou the king of England's eyes!" That prayer was answered when a king ordered the publication of the Bible in English. We might well pray that America's eyes be opened to the message of the Bible. God speaks to this nation in its hour of trial. Let God be heard, and we shall be together as a people. It is spiritual unity that makes for national solidarity.

The present does not seem to care enough about the religious experience of the past. The genuine "old-time religion" was not mere profession, but the whole life in Christian thought and conduct. A spiritual people founded this nation in righteousness. All for which our fathers lived and died can be lost in our own lives. A world of blasphemous dictators and complacent democracies is a hard and dangerous world. Physical isolation has been proved impossible for America, but spiritual leadership among the nations would have been practical. Uncle Sam needs to repent of sin that is a reproach to any people. In our national life there has been a steady drift from the faith of our fathers, and from our fathers' God. *A bigger threat than fifth columnists in our midst is the inner enemies of the spirit. The invasion we have most to fear is the invasion of sin. We should be on guard against sabotage in religion. Godlessness can bring America to judgment, and Godliness can save America to the blessing of oncoming generations.* O "praise the Power that hath made and preserved us a nation!"

The Bible has not been destroyed. It is still a lamp and a light for the path of wisdom and right. Knowledge of what it contains is a requisite of the truly educated life. Its teachings are most dependable. It is infallible in its message of salvation, instruction in living, and guidance under God.

"The Truth Shall Make You Free"

The Bible is a lamp and a light for human freedom. *God's Book will outlast "Mein Kampf."* We have taken our liberty for granted when millions of people have lost theirs. We seem too little concerned about America's neglect of the Bible. We remain free only in its truth. I have seen this quotation from Mussolini: "Liberty is dead, and its corpse is already putrescent." Hitler imprisons the Bible Christians in concentration camps. Stalin has long been in his campaign against God. The religious nationalism of Japan is not good for that nation or for religion. The Bible stands for human liberty. It looks upon the enemies of human freedom as the ultimate losers. It also warns the

possessors of freedom that they can lose it too. The
Bible keeps alive the hope of freedom in the hearts
of the persecuted and conquered peoples. It also
warns against moral collapse among free men. The
times are opportune for a new appreciation and use
of the Bible, so vitally related to the American way
of life. The Lord keep us a "sweet land of liberty,"
and shining "freedom's holy light"! Religion can go
on without democracy, but democracy cannot go on
without religion.

The tyranny of sin enslaves men. To be free from
sin is the ideal freedom. It underlies all other freedom worth the name. Nations are sinners before God.
Freedom has been used as an occasion to the flesh.
We have not served one another in love, but worked
to the undoing of brotherhood. The whole world
shares a common guilt. The Bible has gone unheeded.
"Stand fast therefore in the liberty wherewith Christ
hath made us free." The Biblical condition has not
been met. "If the Son therefore shall make you free,
ye shall be free indeed." Only he could say: "*I am
. . . . the truth*"—the truth that sets men free.

"The Light of Men"

"These are written, that ye might believe that
Jesus is the Christ, the Son of God; and that believing
ye might have life through his name." And "in him
was life; and the life was the light of men." From
Genesis to Revelation—the pre-eminence of Jesus! The
fulfillment of law and prophecy! The Christ of his-

tory and experience! That light will not go out. The Bible has not been destroyed.

J. D. Jones sees the permanent element in religion as our common love and devotion to the person of our Lord. That makes us akin to the saints and pioneers of every age. To have this happy and profitable fellowship will cause us to store up the Bible within. The Bible is the Book of Life, and makes known the Life-Giver. We need a reaffirmation of the Bible. When his people turned to a reading of the Bible, John Richard Green, British historian, wrote: "No greater moral change ever passed over a nation." In that religious classic, *Pilgrim's Progress*, Christian on his way up Hill Difficult lost his scroll. Further progress was checked until he returned and recovered it. O people! we have lost the Bible from our lives. We cannot climb Hill Difficult without it. We must return to God's word. Let us preach its searching truths in the pulpit. Let us hear its saving truths in the pew.

We repeat after thee, O psalmist, "Thy word is a lamp unto my feet and a light unto my path." We borrow the verse of a modern psalmist, Alfred Grant Walton:

> Thou art a blazing sun whose warming light
> Still dries the dew of penitential tears,
> Gives life to all the world, makes clear the sight,
> The power of truth, the Love that conquers fears.
> O Book of Books, our Lamp, our Flame, our Sun,
> Reveal! Refine! Inspire! till heaven is won.

V

THE CHURCH STILL STANDS

Life's Breaking Point

As GUEST preacher in a New York pulpit, Dr. John Hutton preached one Sunday morning from the interesting topic, "Life's Breaking Point." Among his comforting words to be remembered were these: "In a world like this, which is not forsaken by God, you never know what good is waiting around the corner." A burdened young man sat in the congregation. He had seen the topic advertised, and come to hear the sermon for his own need. A few days before his intended bride had met sudden death. His sense of loss was heavy. Life had tumbled in. His faith was wavering. He was finding it hard to carry on. Now came the preacher's word of certainty and assurance. The young man left the House of Prayer to face life anew with a determined trust. He found the corner, and turned it, and FOUND GOD.

The Christian religion must meet life at the breaking point and prevent its going to pieces. For that reason the church still stands. The church holds on to the worth of life, and is a shining lamp in the darkness. It is the one light to which men will turn as long as the cross towers o'er the wrecks of time. Said Jesus to his own: *"Ye are the light of the world."*

Poet Edwin Markham has sung of the sustaining faith that makes the church necessary for these times:

> At the heart of the cyclone tearing the sky
> And flinging the clouds and the towers by,
>   Is a place of central calm;
> So here in the roar of mortal things,
> I have a place where my spirit sings,
>   In the hollow of God's palm.

The Worship of God

The church still stands as the light of the world in its call to worship God. It was the opinion of Emerson that no greater calamity could befall a nation than the loss of worship. It is true that church doors are no longer open in some sections of our warring world. It is true that wayside shrines have felt the weight of bombs. The powers of darkness have exacted their toll of the holy places. But the church is more than a physical building. It is a light that burns in the spirit of man. It is a light that burns underground in modern Europe as it burned in the catacombs of ancient Rome.

What about our own land? In the absence of dictators and persecution, we have voluntarily closed churches and shamefully neglected them. Although much of our leadership has come from the countryside, many rural fields are left to grow in weeds. Many rural populations are unchurched. Some of our churches have fallen into the hands of fanatical sects, and those whom we should have served are swept from us on a tide of wild emotionalism.

Empty pews cry out against us. There has been

an alarming decline in attendance upon the appointed means of grace. The latest available figures indicated that only one half of the church membership consistently attends the services. A brilliant writer in a magazine of large circulation asserts that America cannot be called Christian with one man out of nine going to church. A prominent radio minister declares that the Sunday evening hour is gone in one third of the churches. *The Christian Advocate* pleads for the restoration of the midweek prayer meeting.

If only one prayer could be made for a nation at war, it would not be wasted effort to pray for a penitent return of our people to the worship of Almighty God. There, before the altar of the Most High, life would bow down to know heaven's beauty touching this ugly, battle-scarred earth. Life would rise up to know that it is not rooted in time and sense and matter. Life would go forth in the help of the Lord against the hosts of evil. Some say that the church will be filled again with worshipers, and that a spiritual awakening of world proportions is near. Let that be our hope. But no great revival of religion came out of the old World War. There was instead spiritual indifference and moral collapse. And no revival will come out of this second World War unless God gets more attention!

Unbelief is strongly organized in its rebellion against God. A university professor has said: "There is absolutely no reason to doubt that man is capable of going on happily and sanely without any sense of dependence upon God, and without any apprehension of cosmic support." Such is the wisdom of the world that God confounds. *Man cannot handle life alone.* That evidence is not lacking now. Man cannot live contentedly in a purposeless universe. He has a deep heart hunger for the Bread of Life. His mental clouds need to be dispersed by the Sun of Righteousness. His life's ills need the healing of the Great Physician. The worship of God is absolutely necessary to the individual and to the nation. The church still stands to keep alive for man the sense of the Eternal.

> If the chosen soul could never be alone
> In deep mid-silence, open-doored to God,
> No greatness ever had been dreamed or done.

From the hard pressures and increasing tensions of today's living man wants release. From the tempests that sweep down upon him he wants a place of refuge and rest and peace. When burdens are heavy and problems perplexing he wants strength and understanding. Threatened with fears and sick with worries he wants courage and faith. With standards falling all about him he wants a secure grip. With foundations crumbling beneath him he wants a sure footing. O man! worship God. Wrote Longfellow:

> So, as I enter here from day to day,
>   And leave my burden at this minster gate,
> Kneeling in prayer, and not ashamed to pray,
>   The tumult of the time disconsolate
> To inarticulate murmurs dies away,
>   While the eternal ages watch and wait.

After thirty-three years of preaching on Broadway, Charles E. Jefferson said: "We must quit playing at

63

religion and listen to God." It is in the act of worship
that life listens. *God has something to say*. We have
need to be still and know that he is God. It was a
notion of Pascal that many human ills spring from an
inability to sit still in a room. What would he think
now? Moderns "go places and do things." Days are
hurried through. Living is fast. Patience is soon exhausted. Shouting and screaming replace conversation. The schedule of life needs revision. We ought
to take time out and worship God. The church still
stands to call us to a recognition of his worth.

The Meeting with Christ

The church is the light of the world in its ex-
altation of Christ. He gave origin to the church, and
the church must be loyal to its Founder. He bestowed
his Spirit upon the church, and the church must be
strong in that power. He sent the church forth to
evangelize a world, and the church must not fail him
in that service of souls.

Christ promises to meet with people wherever and
whenever they are assembled in his name. What a
holy privilege to meet with Christ! One has been
thrilled in meeting with personalities of renown. Here
is the thrill of thrills—meeting with Christ! Here is
life's highest calling: "Follow me." Here is life's
exacting question: "What do ye more than others?"

If we are met with Christ, we come to know his
claims upon our discipleship. One claim will be that
of *distinction*. Another will be the *pledge of first*

allegiance. Still another will be the *willingness to serve*. The world is hindered by those who show no difference in conduct, divide their loyalties, and have no passion for souls. The church still stands to measure discipleship by the ministry of Jesus Christ. It will not take down the cross from its costly position in the gospel. So indelibly has that position been stamped on life that the average sinner will unhesitatingly state his expectations of the Christian. O my people, we must witness for our living Lord! Witnessed the Calvinist to the king of France: "It belongs to the church of God, whereof I am an unworthy minister, rather to receive blows than give them; but your majesty will remember that it is an anvil that hath broken many hammers."

Christ spoke to his disciples at a time of crisis: "Let not your heart be troubled." The world is in trouble, and may find comfort in the Christian faith. "Ye believe in God, believe also in me." Faith in the person of Christ is a light in the darkness. He has lived the life of conquest. He has turned back the tempter. He has cast out the devils. He has healed the sick. He has caused the dead to live. He has calmed the storm. He has found the lost. He has brought peace. He has endured hardship. He has suffered pain. He has faced opposition. He has experienced struggle. Out of his triumph and power, and with the promise of his sufficient grace, Christ speaks to us. He is the grand adequacy of the gospel.

The Privilege of Prayer

The church is the light of the world in its invitation
to prayer. It points to the unshaken Throne of Grace
when the thrones of men are giving way. It gives
freedom of expression to the spirit when the bodies of
men are denied their liberties. Bomb and burn the
churches, but worshipers pray to keep kindled their
light of devotion and communion! As long as one
church steeple reaches for the sky, so long will man
kneel in prayer. If his last temple were to be destroyed, he would yet pray for the temple not made
with hands. Life has need of prayer. Prayer brings
us to face ourselves, makes us dependent on other
power, humbles us to do the holy will, puts the world's
burdens on our shoulders, and bids us see life through.

Much modern thought is allied against prayer.
Many do not care to see themselves as they are. They
are slow in admitting their helplessness. They want
their own way about things. They question God's
concern in world events. They assume no responsibility for others. They give emphasis to the futility
of life. Prayer has been dismissed as unsound and
unscientific. But across the years the saints have
found profit in prayer. They have had mended the
breaks in life. They have had tears dried. They have
had faith renewed. They have tapped fresh sources
of strength. They have had rebirth of hope. They
have had the victories of love. The saints have known
that "more things are wrought by prayer than this
world dreams of."

Prayer is not automatic. We must prepare ourselves to pray.

Prayer is not magic. It is contact with God.

Prayer is not selfishness. It is seeking first the kingdom of God, and sharing it with others.

Prayer is not telling God "where to get off." It is telling God to come in.

Prayer is not expecting God to do everything. It is personal co-operation with him to get things done.

Prayer is not satisfying speech to an audience of self. It is hard wrestling with the angel of the Lord for a blessing.

Prayer is not asking for a violation of God's laws. It is asking that we be brought into obedience to them.

Prayer is not easy sentiment. Prayer is hard realism of Gethsemane's agony and Calvary's sacrifice.

Life is gloriously meant to know God. We are to live in his Son. We are to be led by his Spirit. By the beliefs of our hearts we are to be saved unto righteousness. By the work of our hands we are to serve humanity. We are to offer ourselves a living sacrifice unto the Lord. When life thus measures up, unceasing prayer will produce spiritual leadership and successful discipleship. And these terrific days are in great need of both.

Prayer Is Heard and Answered

God hears and answers prayer. The church still stands for that realization in experience. What we call unanswered prayer is often God's refusal to conform to some unwise desire. *Prayer must always be willing for God to be God!* He knows what is best for us and the common good. The mother of Augustine prayed that her son might not go to Rome. He did go, and was converted. Although the mother was not permitted to fix the geographical boundary of God's work, a fond longing of her motherly soul was met. And her boy had to pray through to victory over a besetting sin. He too found God's perfect way in prayer.

This little verse by Ethel Romig Fuller has helped my preaching and been requested by many walks of life:

> If radio's slim fingers
>   Can pluck a melody
> From night, and toss it over
>   A continent, or sea;
>
> If the petaled white notes
>   Of a violin
> Are blown across a mountain,
>   Or a city's din;
>
> If songs, like crimson roses,
>   Are culled from thin blue air,
> Why should mortals wonder
>   If God hears prayer?

Prayer tunes in to God. Prayer makes life receptive to his presence. The day of miracles is not ended. God continues his wonderful works of grace in human nature. Men made over again become the lights of the world. The church still stands to shine. Prayer is necessary to salvation. We can pray. Let us pray.

Let the Church Be the Church

The church is the light of the world in its gospel. Its ministry is that of the written and living word. Ruskin thought that the issues of life and death are in the pulpit. These issues are also in the pew. We are called to be both hearers and doers of the word of God. The gospel is good news for a weary world. We are called to spread it. The gospel is Christ. We are called to live him. The desirable combination for the church is an evangel in the pulpit, and a redeemed membership in the pew. Then the revivals will come. Souls will be born into the kingdom, and be added to the church.

It is recorded that, when the early Christians stood before the church at Antioch, "they rehearsed all that God had done *with* them, and how he had opened the door of faith unto the Gentiles." What has God done with us? What doors has he opened through us for others? "To think of today's work as a part of the infinite work is an immortal's habit," said Everett Hale. Working together with God is life's highest honor, and eternity's fame. The church still stands for the high calling in Christ. There is a task for the Christian servant and friend. This age has plenty of horsepower, but God is short of manpower. Man in the hands of God will put a machine age back in the control of man. That is the way to get the Spirit in the wheels.

When Matthew Arnold was low of spirit, he knelt in Rugby Chapel. There his father had preached.

There lay the sacred dust, a treasure of the earth. There vision came with strength to get up and go again. We may have radiant communion with the invisible company of the saints! That is not the least of the possessions of the church. "The memory of the just is blessed." As others have blessed us, we too can be a blessing.

Since Jesus Came

The world is not the same since Jesus came. In the light of his coming the world is either judged or saved. That is also true of the church. Would we know about the love of God? Listen to Jesus. Would we know about a brotherhood of saved men? Listen to Jesus. Would we know about the new world order? Listen to Jesus. "All authority hath been given unto me in heaven and on earth. Go ye therefore, and make disciples of all the nations, baptizing them into the name of the Father and of the Son and of the Holy Spirit: teaching them to observe all things whatsoever I commanded you: and lo, *I am with you always, even unto the end of the world.*"

Nineteen centuries of history, and the church still stands. Its light has not gone out. Conflict is nothing new for the church. In loyalty to its Lord it must be at conflict with sin. True to its origin it does not fear the return of the Caesars. Crises are nothing new for the church. The background of world events is indeed dark, but in the foreground is the cross. By that sign we conquer. There is the Power that makes

for righteousness among men. Empires pass and are
no more, but the kingdom is coming!

> Be the banner still unfurled,
>   Still unsheathed the Spirit's sword
> Till the kingdoms of the world
>   Are the kingdom of the Lord.

VI

MAN IS OF ETERNAL WORTH

What Is Man?

WHAT IS man? "The ancient question is the modern crisis." The question has been answered to the impoverishment of life. Some have answered that man is everything. That is not true. Others have answered that man is nothing. That is not true either. Between these extremes of thought there is the right answer. A true conception of human personality takes in God. Said Carlyle: "The older I grow, and I now stand on the brink of eternity, the more there comes back to me the first sentence in the catechism which I learnt as a child, and the fuller and deeper its meaning becomes: 'What is the chief end of man? to glorify God and enjoy him forever.'"

All depends on what man thinks of himself. Human values have not been conserved in this wasteful age of sin. Theories of inevitable progress, kingdoms of selfish power, and lowered moral standards have crushed out the holier meanings of man.

Man ought to be on life's main road with God, and filled with a grand sense of his intended destiny. A verse in Proverbs reads: *"The path of the just is as the shining light, that shineth more and more unto the perfect day."* This road on which God walks with man is open, and it is not necessary to use the world's detours. The eternal worth of man is a shining lamp in the darkness. Light falls on the straight and narrow way.

Man is more than a physical being. There is a spirit in man.

Man is more than a puppet. He is called to be a living witness of the gospel.

Man is more than a victim of the machine. He is raised up to be the master of wheels.

Man is more than an instrument of the state. He has his individual rights, by the grace of God, to brotherhood and freedom.

Man is more than a cold figure in an economic process. He does not live by bread alone. There is also a hunger after righteousness.

Man is more than a product of ancestry and environment. He can overcome both in the triumph of redeemed character.

Man is more than a cosmic accident, "a disease on the surface of our planet." He can realize his personal relationship as a child of God and experience daily divine love and blessing.

Man is more than a helpless creature of cruel fate destined at last to be "blown across the desert dust or sealed within the iron hills." His soul goes marching on.

What is man? Let us hear and hold the Christian answer. Man is the crowning work of God's creation. He is the citizen of two worlds here to help enthrone Jesus Christ. Man is not a world ruler. He cannot take the place of our Lord. Judgment and history are against the superman. Man's best living is done in the realm of the spiritual. His soundest value is belonging unto God. He is a being of eternal worth. His testimony is to ring with the truth of redemption. Only then does he have complete mastery over himself. Only then does he love his kind. Only then does he enjoy and appreciate freedom. Only then is his soul's hunger gratified. Only then is life's victory assured. Only then is truly possessed the hope of immortality. Only then does man express the beginning of eternal life. There is "SOMETHING OTHER" inside, and the Holy Spirit bears witness with the human spirit to sonship in the kingdom.

> Chief of all thy wondrous works,
>   Supreme of all thy plan,
> Thou hast put the upward reach
>   Into the heart of man.

A High Opinion of Oneself

Man's eternal worth consists in serving God's eternal purpose. He is created for God's glory. Here is sanctified individualism. It is the spiritual quality that distinguishes life. Only as man works co-operatively with God is humanity helped onward. We have grievously sinned in working unto ourselves. We have violated the written law of our creation. We have not lived out the definition of character. We have substituted a bold, wicked egotism for a humble, converted self-esteem. Today's mad world sees ruthless dictators mowing down men without any regard for the sacredness of personality. But that tragic fact alone is not the modern scene. The headlines are tragic because lifelines have made them possible. Professedly Christian nations have used life without any regard for the Creator and Saviour of souls.

In common sin the world has lost the dignity of being. We have made an evil environment encouraging to war and the totalitarian state. There seems to be lacking a spiritual unity for the defense of democracy. Whatever else may divide them, the militarist and pacifist see together one sign of the times— *democracy is in danger of its life.* The Christian sees the absolute necessity for the guidance and help of God.

An old Edinburgh weaver prayed: "O God, help me to hold a high opinion of myself." Byron wrote to a friend: "Virtue, I begin to see, is the only thing which will do in this damned world." Whether one prays to hold on to what he has, or realizes what he has lost, man must live with himself. That self is in need of a clear record. That self needs a heart of purity, and a conscience without stain. That self needs adjustment to life's sacredness.

> Couldst thou in vision see
>   The man God meant,
> Thou never more wouldst be
>   The man thou art, content.

To hold a high opinion of oneself is to walk in the path of the just. There is light on the way of the good man. He seeks daily to do the will of his

God. He presses forward to the goal of his perfection in Christ.

"Behold the Man!"

The words of Pontius Pilate are among the most unforgettable utterances of time. He confessed his inability to find any fault in Jesus. The servant of the state told the truth concerning the Perfect Man. He was made to raise the cross above the flag of empire. He was made to acknowledge the way of the righteous preferable to that of the Caesars. Even he, one of the worst sinners, caught the gleam of manhood in the Galilean. That light brought its own judgment upon Pilate's dark decision to surrender Jesus to the crowd.

Jesus made man at home in the universe. He gave reality to the religious experience of the cosmic God. He wrote across the face of the whole universe, "from stars to grass," the word "Father." All human values were conserved in that extraordinary life lived among ordinary men. Jesus was positive of the fatherhood of God. In a universe of agony he was sure of it. He was not unmindful of the happenings that tried people's souls. But he pointed with the simplicity of faith to a fallen bird, an unfolding lily, a drop of water, the grasses of the field, a lost sheep. Man was of eternal worth to the Maker and Shepherd of human life. That teaching was at Calvary. For when Jesus died with men doing their worst to him, he cried in his last words: "Father, forgive them. . . . ."

I have sailed with my father in stormy seas, but was

unafraid with him at the helm of the ship. There was a laddie's confidence in his father's presence amid wind and wave. How much more can God be trusted by his children! Man is safe in the storms of life if he knows that God is at the helm. Even if the ship goes down, man may still be in the hands of God. We should never forget this truth: *the good is as real as the bad*. We are twisted in our thought when we give reality to the bad and turn aside from the fact of the good. GOD LOVES US! Whatever happens, that is true.

Jesus taught God's truth about life. He lived God's life in the flesh. He headed life in God's direction. His consciousness of God, emphasis on Saviourhood, and the salvation of character are the supreme essentials for our times.

The Incarnation closely associates God with humanity. Dr. Gordon commented: "The coming of Jesus means the awakening of humanity to its ideal and divine side. To reject him is equivalent to the expulsion of the divine from human thought and concern. Humanity stands or falls with the acceptance of Christ its king." Christ took upon himself our fallen nature, represented mankind, and atoned for the guilt of the race.

The one tendency of Christ is to lift man heavenward. There is a magnetic pull in his gospel. It raises man to higher ground. It sets pilgrim feet in the path of the just. It tugs at the eternity in the heart. It puts splendor on the horizon of the pilgrimage. It holds us in faith and hope and love. The abundant life in Christ makes us sons of God. "Now are we the sons of God, and it doth not yet appear what we shall be: but we know that, when he shall appear, we shall be like him; for we shall see him as he is."

We are!

We shall be!

We shall see him!

O Man,

> Turn your eyes upon Jesus,
>   Gaze full in his wondrous face,
> And the things of earth will grow strangely dim
>   In the light of his glory and grace.

"Shew Thyself a Man"

Man is of eternal worth in the goodness and faithfulness of his character. The "well done" of the Master is the great reward of the Christian life. That life is one of wholeminded and wholehearted service. We are to be good and faithful in our several callings. The world would differ in its idea of greatness. It often sneers at goodness. It often belittles fidelity. The world strives after temporal fame, indulges in the pleasures of flesh, and rebels against discipline.

The modern conceit is thinking that we are entitled to change the rules of living. Who are we? The same in our human natures as men who lived before us. Beneath the surface of our changing world is the fact of unchanged man. Only God in Christ can change human nature. Moderns face the old experiences, old problems, old questions. The victories, solutions, answers lie within. Man needs—more than all else—the forgiveness of sin. Dr. C. G. Jung, psychologist of note, in his *Modern Man in Search of a Soul*, wrote: "During the past thirty years people from all the civilized countries of the earth have consulted me. . . . . Among my patients in the second half of life—that is to say, those over thirty-five—there has not been one whose problem in the last resort was not that of finding a religious outlook on life. It is safe to say that every one of them fell ill because he had lost that which the living religions of every age have given to their followers, and none of them has been really healed who did not regain his religious outlook."

> . . . . I need, now as then,
> Thee, God, who mouldest men.

In an old book there is a man who had a mania for building towers. He succeeded at last in building one tower with eleven thousand stairs. Just as he was ready to congratulate himself upon his accomplishment, *he looked up and saw the stars*. Man cannot build beyond God! We cannot build unto ourselves, and get by. To build life with God is the eternal worth of man. The colossal failure of man is the failure to do what is right.

"What Shall It Profit a Man . . . . ?"

Physical and mental man is breaking down. He has lived and thought for the things that perish. Jesus once asked: "What shall it profit a man, if he shall gain the whole world and lose his own soul? Or what shall a man give in exchange for his soul?" God knows the multitudes of his stars and sands.

79

But God has no given figures for reckoning the value of a single soul. Such is the eternal worth he has placed upon man. And man ought to live like an immortal.

> Life is real! Life is earnest!
>   And the grave is not its goal;
> Dust thou art, to dust returnest,
>   Was not spoken of the soul.

When man loses sight of his soul, he cannot expect to be treated like a spiritual being. The world is stricken with that blindness, and life is plunged into a midnight of blood. Man has sought to gain the world at the awful cost of his own personality. Racial superiority, economic injustice, political corruption, social immorality, lost freedom, destructive nationalism —these are evidences of a sin-marked age. These are not, however, the only marks. Certain expressions of popular science, philosophies of material success, and teachings in humanistic religion have tended to lower man's dignity. Man, just an animal! Man, just a bundle of instincts and complexes! Man, with desires that must be gratified! Man, existent for pleasure and comfort and money! Man, lifting himself out by his own bootstraps to a new world!

O saving Christ, our Light and our Life, call us back to the path of the just!

Redemption and Conviction

Fallen man can be lifted. The sinner can become a saint. Redemption restores man to a conviction of his eternal worth. He is willing to make amends to

God, and be made over. Declared Henry Ward Beecher: "The church that cannot sing 'Jesus, Lover of My Soul' deserves to die." But the church does sing that song in the night. It has the needful message for man. Man cannot be his own saviour. There is One who saves. Man cannot "pluck from the memory a rooted sorrow," nor "raze out the written troubles of the brain." He must be cleansed of his iniquities through forgiveness. There is forgiveness of sins with God.

A Welsh evangelist exclaimed in his sermon: "O heaven! heaven! thy walls would be empty enough were not the church on earth mothering sons for thee!" Let the church hold fast to that task. We must not despair of man. We must not lose our faith in human possibilities *plus divine grace*. Give man another chance to repent of what he has done and been. Encourage him to belief in Christ's way of life. Provide by passionate prayer and love and service a favorable atmosphere for spiritual revival.

"The path of the just is as the shining light, that shineth more and more unto the perfect day." A lighted path! An increasing light! The glorious dawning! "Ye are come . . . . to the spirits of just men made perfect"! At home with God!

VII

LIFE IS WORTH LIVING

God's Luminaries

WHEN REDEEMED man comes to know his eternal worth, he comes to know also that life is worth living. When times are darkest a son of God shines. He has worked out his own salvation with fear and trembling before the Lord. He has yielded his will to a higher Will. He takes fresh hold on the word of Life. Others seeing the lesser light of human example find their way to a greater light which is Christ.

In the distressful night of sin now fallen upon humanity, God must have his luminaries. For men are everywhere losing faith in life. They are letting go the old convictions. They break established traditions. They give up holy ideals. They surrender to defeatism and cynicism. Many feel with Cowper that life is

> A painful passage o'er a restless flood,
> A vain pursuit of fugitive false good,
> A scene of fancied bliss and heartfelt care,
> Closing at last in darkness and despair.

The apostle Paul in his epistle to the Philippians spoke the truth of Christian experience. *"The sons of God, ... ye shine as lights in the world; holding forth the word of life."* Paul has known the worst of life, but still believes in the best. He has seen the conquest of sin, but still expects the triumph of right. He has been beset by opposition of men, but has remained loyal to the mission of Christ. He will not let the darkness get him down, but will stand up to life in the light of his salvation. He will not be overcome by things as they are, but will shine for the things that ought to be. God's man—a shining lamp in the darkness! A light for the purpose of life!

Life Is a Gift

Life is worth living when we accept it, and use it, as the gift of God. The gift of his thoughtfulness toward us. The gift to be treasured as coming from our truest Friend. The gift to stir up our hearts in loving remembrance of him.

When a noted artist committed suicide, an editorial carried this terse comment: "He was a successful artist, with editors eager to snatch paper from beneath his pencil, but he found life emptier than do the men in the breadlines." People do find life empty. There is a failure in success. There is a vacancy in the soul. And men have walked in the breadlines because moderns have hoarded or wasted the plenty of God's goodness. Life has been earthbound when the spirit wanted to soar.

God thinks of us. *None other than a personal God will do.* The old emphasis on Providence may have disappeared largely from the pulpit, but the fact of Providence needs to be realized in the pew. One recalls the good minister of his youth announcing future services with that serious introduction: "Providence permitting, ..." If anything should happen to upset human plans before meeting again at church, God could be trusted. He knew best. Let men carry that conviction from worship to their labors. A man can keep his chin up when he feels that he does count in life. Living under the watchful eye of Providence, he will take life more seriously. And there just is not any other way to take life!

God is our friend. That calls for our friendship in return. It is one of the finest insights of Scripture that "a friend loveth at all times." Whatever may come to pass, God loves us still. We are to love him too under all conditions. By this fellowship and love we "shine as lights in the world; holding forth the word of life." Robert Louis Stevenson did not meet James Chalmers until the latter had become an old man. Said Stevenson regretfully: "I have come to love you too late." O how many of us do not love God soon enough! We are beaten by circumstances because we did not realize his friendly presence. We are not prepared for hard struggle because we did not avail ourselves of his help. There would be far less difficulty with the reverses of life if we went ahead more with our opportunities to know God. He will love and keep us in the worth of life.

> They err who say life is not sweet,
> Though cares are long, and pleasures fleet;
> Through smiles and tears, and sun and storms,
> Still change life's ever-varying forms.
> The mind that looks on things aright,
> Sees through the clouds God's deep blue light.

We are to remember God in friendship to mankind. If we are the sons of God, we are members of his world family. We must learn how to live and work, love and sing, laugh and weep, *together*. We must pray for, and seek to win, the prodigals from the far country of riotous living. We must try to make human relations right. We must preach salvation to the lost. As the Master's eventful road came nearer its ending, he said to his disciples: "Ye are my friends, if ye do whatsoever I command you."

Life's Holy Cause

Life is worth living when there is a holy cause. Ingersoll's tribute to Lincoln was: "He lived until there remained nothing more for him to do as great as he had done." In Rice's play *Day of Judgment* a judge reminds that it is not enough to know what to live for; one must know also what to die for. The thrilling and adventurous chapters of Christianity are written in the mighty heroisms of personal abandon. Men have answered the call of the cross and given themselves in utmost sacrifice. With a high sense of obligation to the gospel and a first allegiance to their Lord, men have gone willingly and bravely to martyrdom.

Always God has a holy cause for life. He will show us what it is. He will guide us into the doing of it. God still speaks to men and leads them. Life may be in constant touch with him. This age has not outgrown the need for divine revelation and divine guidance.

Always there is something left undone unless we do our appointed task. Others cannot fulfill the mission to which God has called us. Society gains from those who assume the responsibility of discipleship. What we stand for should be light for somebody's darkness. What we give ourselves to should be as the word of life.

In a world like ours there is no dearth of holy causes. Human remedies have failed to cure a sin-sick people. The Great Physician is nigh. We can call attention to his healing ministry for human ills. We can further prove him in the healing of our own lives. Thus we shine as the sons of God in the cure of self, and in the new health of regeneration.

> The healing of the world
> Is in its nameless saints. Each separate star
> Seems nothing, but a myriad scattered stars
> Break up the Night, and make it beautiful.

Getting the Best of Trouble

Life is worth living when trouble is overcome. Dr. Joseph Sizoo thinks that life is too easy for most of us. Dr. Paul Scherer speaks of those who have "woven life's defeats into battleflags, and made them to wave in the winds of misfortune." Life has not been put to a real test until trouble arrives on the scene. Victorious living is determined by how one faces calamity. There is inspiration in the story of that master violin maker who chose the wood for his instruments from the north side of the trees. So it seems that God has chosen his good and faithful servants from life's north side. The winds have blown strong and cold. Taut strings of trial have been drawn across the character of faith. But the Heavenly Musician has brought forth sweetest melody from troubled lives.

If there were removed from the pages of Scripture all those who got the best of trouble, we would lose the names that mean the most.

If history were deprived of all those who overcame their hardships and oppositions, it would be to hinder healing waters in the high tides of thought and action.

If the minister were to lose all those who fought triumphantly against heavy odds, he would be without the living proofs of his gospel.

The deep root of trouble is within. The president of Princeton Seminary had these words in the press: "The chief thraldom in which man finds himself is not bondage to external ills, but bondage to his own evil will." If man is right with God, saved in Christ, empowered by the Holy Spirit, he is able to contend with an antagonistic world. If man is wrong inside, he is already defeated in the struggle of life.

We are to know ourselves. Not until God comes into the picture do we get at a proper understanding of ourselves. He knows our personalities and their differences. He sees what there is in us. Give him a chance to use us, and he will fit us into his plans. He will elevate us to the true dignity of being and the service of character.

We are to accept ourselves. We are not to be tossed about by self-pity. How fatal is that affliction!

We are not to force life into a corner with our self-conceit. The human "I" is not to be substituted for the divine "I AM." We are to answer God's commands in prompt obedience and loyal dedication. No two of the disciples were alike. But the Upper Room needed an absent, doubting Thomas as much as it needed the revived, preaching Peter.

We are to be ourselves. We are to be genuine, and not cheap imitations. We are intended for spiritual freedom, and not satisfaction of sinful desires. Why do men not see in religion the more excellent way to express themselves? Why insist that indulgence in the lusts of flesh is "being alive" and "seeing life"? *Sin is death to personality.*

Worth Going On

Life is worth living when we make it worth going on. The monotony of existence is broken by taking hold of new blessings each day. The commonplace becomes uncommon when the Rose of Sharon blooms. The ordinary task becomes extraordinary when one toils with the Carpenter of Nazareth. One is helped to carry crosses in fellowship with the Redeemer. There is cheer for loneliness when one thinks of the Lonely Christ. There is courage for conflict when one follows after him who never retreated. There is faith for living when one is kept by him who never lost his faith. There is hope for tomorrow when one belongs to him who is the Resurrection and the Life.

The late Clarence Darrow denied that life is worth going on. Shortly before he died, he advised youth to "chuck life away." Yet when that brilliant lawyer addressed the jury of a crowded courtroom, he employed all the talents of his genius to save youth from the "chair" and gallows. Long after Darrow's paraded cynicism is forgotten, his able defenses of life will abide in memory. I believe that underneath the cynicism of today there lies smothered the feeling that life might be worth going on. Dorothy Parker has ably written of that mixed sense of futility and need in the modern scene:

> There's little in taking or giving,
>   There's little in water or wine;
> This living, this living, this living
>   Was never a project of mine.
> Oh, hard is the struggle, and sparse is
>   The gain of the one at the top,
> For art is a form of catharsis,
>   And love is a permanent flop,
> And work is the province of cattle,
>   And rest's for a clam in the shell,
> So I'm thinking of throwing the battle—
>   Would you kindly direct me to hell?

Is it not possible that such testimony can come of an eternal uneasiness within? The heart reaching out for a meaning to life and the universe? Human hope that the good might triumph over wrong? Listening for the assurance of a Voice?

O let the sons of God shine as lights in the world! Let them hold forth the word of life! *We are his project!* Men should find in religion an assistance for their struggles, and the fighting chance to win. Men should find in religion an accurate appraisal of human values. Men should find in religion a progressive experience of God. In such discoveries the soul under stress and strain will know life's permanent worth.

Growing Pains

Life is worth living when there is growth. The power of growth is the miracle of creation and life. Dr. Clovis Chappell uses effectively that illustration of Thomas Carlyle holding a baby in his arms, and exclaiming: "Just to think that Shakespeare was once like this!" Only God is an adequate explanation for it.

We are to grow in mind and heart and soul. Growth will not be free from pain. Sometimes when a laddie's limbs would ache, Mother would say in comforting confidence: "Growing pains will make you a big man." No one remains loyal to the things worth while without paying a dear price. There is a heavy cost in dreaming great dreams. There is ofttimes agony in keeping to the ideal. To grow in favor with God and man is to reproduce the Christ in life. And that means tears and bloody sweat, thorns and nails.

"It doth not yet appear what we shall be." A lifetime is the time for growing in grace. The redeemed man is this earth's finest harvest. Preferable to great riches is the good name. Not counted in the markets of business is the worth of religious influence. To have lived something of Christ's life in the world is to welcome the eventide of light. And in the afterglow of our going others will reach home.

Paul, a son of God, shone. He held forth the word of life. He put real worth into living. He used well

90

God's gift, gave himself to a holy cause, got the best of trouble, endured as seeing the invisible, and grew in grace. Who would challenge the testimony of Paul? "I have fought a good fight, I have finished my course, I have kept the faith." To know that Paul lived at all is to know that he was a Christian. The light of his life comes from a dark period of history, and from an experience of suffering. Will we let him say to us "The sons of God, ... ye shine as lights in the world; holding forth the word of life"?

VIII

LOVE DOES TRIUMPH

Where Is Love?

Leslie Weatherhead has called the modern world a
lunatic asylum. Is there anything that religion can
say to a world gone mad?

Let us not forget that the world has gone mad before and been restored to sanity. Let us not go down
under the weight of current events because people are
questioning again the love of God. We have opportunity now to write our own memorable chapter in
the history of the church. For both past experience
and our present plight argue that God remains on the
scene. It is a good sign of the times that God is in
our thought. When life begins to think seriously about
him, although doubts be prominent, the day of revelation is not far distant. The questions of doubt receive the answers of faith. Religion is proved a necessity in the lives of men. The turning of men to God
is the occasion of spiritual revival.

Listen to these words of Thomas Hardy: "If a way
to the better there be, it exacts a full look at the
worst." Job, servant and friend of God, saw the worst.
For a little while of temptation and trial, ugly clouds
hid God from man. But the sky cleared! Job had
not been forsaken in his suffering! The fresh winds of

certainty swept again through his being. He held up his lamp in the darkness. *"And now men see not the bright light which is in the clouds: but the wind passeth, and cleanseth them."*

Dive bombers have not destroyed the great certainties of humanity's religious foundations.

Mechanized units have not forced into retreat the Captain of our salvation.

Submarines have not torpedoed the "old ship of Zion."

Dictators must reckon still with the Throne set in heaven.

Although Gibraltar be taken we have left the Rock of Ages.

The "war of nerves" will never defeat the strong hearts of good soldiers of the cross.

Love is where God is. And God is where his people are.

"The Greatest Thing in the World"

Love is the greatest thing in the world. Love does triumph because GOD IS LOVE. Unless life holds that powerful and saving conviction, nothing else matters. To know that the greatest thing in the world is even greater in God is indeed a happy knowledge. Here is a comprehensive theology for the whole race. In love, God created. In love, God presides. In love, God reveals. In love, God guides. In love, God forgives. In love, God saves. Life must keep its grip on these supreme facts about God, and not let them go.

As far as human need exists,
  Or echoes call,
Love, limitless, divine, persists
  About us all.

Its pulsing waters never tell
  Of bounding shore;
They surge and roll and rise and swell
  Forevermore.

The Almighty Love does not condone sin, but ever yearns for the sinner. Righteousness is written into the constitution of the universe. God is holy. Man is a sinner out of accord with the highest law of his creation. In God's sight there is but one way for man to live, and that is to live right. If man chooses another way of life, he must take the inevitable consequences. He reaps what he sows. Still God is in love with fallen man. He would lift him to his loving heart, and free him from the guilt and penalty of sin.

In recent days the minister has heard: Why does not God do something about this war? *God has done something!* He has shown life once more that his eternal laws cannot be broken. Life only breaks itself against them. If man sows war he must reap loss and ruin. There is no escaping the judgment of his sin. The question is asked: What about those who believe they are fighting for freedom? Surely there can be no word of condemnation for them. They are not responsible for the situation in which they find themselves. God gave to the nations freedom to choose his way of life. The nations have not so chosen, and all other freedoms are imperiled. We must confess to our sorrow, and may we come to truly repent of it, that the democracies are not innocent of all blame in the world situation. God has not been the basic fact in international relationships. Another question: Is not God on the right side? Yes. Whatever is right will win. This means, however, a victory for the eternal purpose. If hostilities were to cease at once, the real war would not be ended. The conflict of ideas would have to be settled in the realm of the spirit.

A brightness in the clouds of war is that there are things that abide. When Napoleon bombarded Vienna, Beethoven wrote music. Spiritual values will not remain buried under the debris of war. There will be a resurrection. The human spirit will survive. God is a sure defense. The greatest thing in the world will not be overcome by those things without greatness. In the long run, love does triumph. For it is love that redeems and heals. Love comes through, because God endures.

> For the loving worm within its clod
> Were diviner than a loveless god
> Amid his worlds, I will dare to say.

Where Do We Stand?

We do not want God to be indifferent. We just cannot harbor that feeling. God does not want us to be indifferent either. How passionate is our concern for a stricken world? When we pray for divine deliverance, what is the deeper implication of our request? Mere intervention to make life easier for us?

Or prayer to be a people worthy of deliverance?
Mere intervention to end human suffering? Or prayer
to be saved from sin that causes so much of human
distress? "From whence come wars and fightings
among you? come they not hence, even of your lusts
that war in your members?" It is when God's love
is shed abroad in human hearts that life shares in the
service of salvation. God's love found its holiest and
completest expression in the unspeakable gift of Jesus
Christ. God came in him to live with men, and sacrifice supremely for their souls. "God, who commanded the light to shine out of darkness, hath shined
in our hearts, to give the light of the knowledge of
the glory of God in the face of Jesus Christ." At
Calvary man has the chance to see how God loves
him.

The Love of Christ

Love does triumph because Christ loves us. "The
Son of God, who loved *me*, and gave himself for *me*!"
O let that wind of truth cleanse our clouds and usher
in the light! Heaven's redemptive love for sinful
"me"!

The papers have carried pictures of bombed churches
in which the crucifix was not destroyed. Why pub-
lish such pictures? Do they not testify to a lingering
belief that there might be something left in life? What
if that something be the love of Christ! Above all
human hate and brutality and conflict there towers the
strangeness of his love. Love with that strange command of loving one another, and setting that down
as evidence of discipleship. Love with that strange

fact of the cross as essential to world salvation. Love
with that strange program of being good and doing
good in a new world order. Love with that strange
crown of thorns and a borrowed tomb, and yet lord-
ship over force and death. Love with that strange
loyalty of a broken heart and a death of shame, and
yet the life of victory. Man can know the love of
Christ as he appropriates the Christly experience. "I
live; yet not I, but Christ liveth in me," said Paul.
"He that hath the Son hath life," assured John.

> I cannot do it alone,
> The waves run fast and high,
> And the fogs close chill around
> And the light goes out in the sky.
> But I know that we two shall win,
> *Jesus and I.*

In a notable sermon preached before the Baptist
World Congress at Atlanta, Dr. Ohrn, of Norway,
stressed: "Paul knew of no proxy religion. To him
salvation meant first and foremost a personal and individual experience of a personal Saviour who did not
love man in the abstract, but who loved each single
soul; a Saviour who loved him and gave himself for
him as truly as if he, Paul, were the only sinner in the
world to experience the redeeming grace of Christ."
That certain faith in Christ loving them, and dying for
them, made early Christians live and die for him. The
blood of the martyrs became the seed of the church.

The love of Christ makes us responsible to others.
With sins forgiven and life redeemed we are separated
to serve. From Christ we get the passion of soul for

souls. We light our lives with his light. That lighted ministry shines for all human need. For Christ is come to seek and to save that which was lost.

The Love of Disciples

Love does triumph because love alone succeeds in human relations. Wrote Tolstoy: "Men think there are circumstances when one may deal with human beings without love. But there are none. You may deal with things without love. Cut trees, bake bricks, hammer iron, but you cannot deal with men without love." Today's world seems to support that outlook. "Love never faileth" is the plain declaration of Scripture. It is also a promise.

Men are wont to say that love has failed. They write down their cynicism and scatter their literature. But in the suffering of humanity a common brotherhood is born. The fellowship of Christ extends to the uttermost parts of the earth. Times like these touch responsive chords in many hearts. When the clouds are gone it will be seen that love has ministered. Sharing the weepings and burdens of humanity is love's creative and redemptive act. It is the practical side of an effective personal Christianity. It is listening to him who said: "Inasmuch as ye have done it unto one of the least of these my brethren, ye have done it unto me"; and, "By this shall all men know that ye are my disciples, if ye have love one to another."

How are we to love? We are to love others even as he has loved us. After attendance at worship two men engaged in conversation concerning the sermon.

"What do you think of Spurgeon?" asked one. Came the surprising reply, "Nothing." And then, "All I can think of is the preacher's Saviour." So may we witness unto so great salvation. That is life's best testimony. A popular business slogan is "Say it with flowers." This ought to be the popular slogan for Christians, "Say it with Christ." He is God's word for all.

Love is not stopped by the possible cost of its service. Love is not exhausted by the burdens it bears. Love is patient in waiting on the Lord. Love is the eloquence of the heart. Love is the motive of good deeds. Love is the discipline of life. Love is the education of character. Love is the influence of the soul.

"Thou shalt love the Lord thy God. . . . . This is the first and great commandment. And the second is like unto it, Thou shalt love thy neighbour as thyself." Sin is a denial of love. It hardens hearts, and makes men brutal. It chokes life with selfishness. It stains life with immorality. It breaks life with hatreds. It turns life against religion. It loses life to its high calling and purpose. Love is the universal language that all men verily understand. That language is spoken by new hearts. We come to love people for the souls they are. We can never disarm in a world of armed hearts. It is useless to talk of a just and enduring peace and carry over the things of war. Love is the spiritual and personal force that changes society only when it has first changed its individual members.

In a Lenten book of the English Bishop Crotty there

is a story illustrative of social transformation. A clergyman was very busy in his study, and was interrupted often by his little daughter. Rather than ask her to leave the room, he cut out a map of Europe in small pieces for her to put back together. Sooner than he expected the work was done. He heard his daughter say: "Daddy, there was a picture of a man on the other side, and when I got the man right, the map came right." *Man right with God! Man right with the whole world!* The lack of enough personal righteousness accounts for the world's wrongs. The pieces of life can be put back together only as men love each other.

The Test of Life

Love does triumph because love makes something of us. "Without love I am nothing." Love puts life to the test. Jesus tested Peter: "Lovest thou me?" Here the word for love is the strongest that could be used. Jesus knew well what love could do for that blundering, impulsive, falling, but eager follower. Once save him to the personal allegiance of first love, and he would shine as a servant of his Lord. The winds of Pentecost would come and sweep through the being of the church. Clouds of despair would be cleansed and the Upper Room flooded with light.

Life will be remembered for its much loving. Love is immortal. After all that love has done, we owe a full measure of devotion to life. That devotion will mark character, show the example of faith at work, inspire decision, and come into destiny. The

43663

certainty of triumph is possessing life in love. It will win at the long last. We have that life to live. Countee Cullen has encouraging lines for life's devotion and triumph:

> I have a rendezvous with Life,
> In days I hope will come,
> Ere youth has sped, and strength of mind,
> Ere voices sweet grow dumb.
> I have a rendezvous with Life,
> When Spring's first heralds hum.
> Sure some would cry it's better far
> To crown their days with sleep
> Than face the road, the wind and rain,
> To heed the calling deep.
> Though wet nor blow nor space I fear,
> Yet fear I deeply, too,
> Lest Death should meet and claim me ere
> I keep Life's rendezvous.

IX

DEATH DOES NOT HAVE THE LAST WORD

The Death of Death

DEATH HAS LOST its sting and the grave its victory in the resurrection of our Saviour Jesus Christ. He could not be held within the sealed tomb of empire. Death was unable to write *finis* to his life. After the blackout of Calvary there came the dawn and light in the Garden. Since then humanity has had a more radiant hope of immortality. The Risen Christ lives forevermore! And that foundation stone of the Christian gospel holds the most comforting of all promises to life: "Because I live, ye shall live also." That is a shining lamp in the darkness. Lift it high, O my soul!

Death is everywhere present in this dying world. Earth knows first hand the fact of death with the "tribes that slumber in its bosom." The nation knows the nearness of death with its "purple testament of bleeding war." The home knows the loneliness of death with its

> . . . . Mother, praying God will save
> Thy sailor—while thy head is bow'd,
> His heavy-shotted hammock-shroud
> Drops in his vast and wandering grave

The drama *Death Takes a Holiday* shocks in its

theme. Death is pictured as taking time out to go around among men and see what they think of him. He discovers that without exception men behold him in paralyzing fear. Life is afraid of him.

Death has met its match in the Son of God! So announces Paul in his letter to Timothy: *"Our Saviour Jesus Christ . . . . hath abolished death, and hath brought life and immortality to light through the gospel."* HE LIVES, AND DEATH IS DEAD!

The Voice of God

Death does not have the last word because God speaks. His presence gives answer to the soul-born question: "If a man die, shall he live again?" God cannot ignore the ageless longing of man. He cannot push aside this cherished hope of his creation. For God has made life with the inner longing and hope for life beyond the grave. The Father of Everlasting Love cannot let his children go. This earth is not all that he has for them. He has something better further on. He can be trusted to bring his people to their abiding place. Death will not hinder the walk with him. Death will only be an interruption. The end of life's road will connect with the golden streets of the New Jerusalem. In the simple spiritual our fathers sang, "Ole Jordan runs between." Studdert-Kennedy beautifully said: "There is in the heart of God, and always has been, a cross and an empty tomb."

God's voice is eternal in the resurrection of Jesus. The character of God is upheld by that historic fact and mighty event of human experience. No one now has good reason to doubt the integrity of God, nor to question his promises. That death was more than God could handle was unthinkable to Old Testament saints. That God did handle death successfully was the urgent and marching conviction of New Testament Christians.

God speaks the words of life to today's dying world. It does not look on the surface of things as if death has been abolished. This world of deathly evidence seems contradictory. But men will not be still and know that God is God. Sin may furnish plentiful evidence for the power of death. The gospel, however, has a greater power. For the living God in Christ is able to destroy sin and save sinners. Humanity has rejected its Saviour "who hath abolished death, and hath brought life and immortality to light through the gospel." Eternal life in the midst of time is the gift of God. Marvelous gift it is, and accepting any other gift in preference of it is not good sense. Death does not, and cannot, defeat the possessor of eternal life.

A soldier, killed in action during World War I, left behind him this reasoning in verse:

> If it be all for naught, for nothingness
> At last, why does God make the world so fair?
> Why spill this golden splendor out across
> The western hills, and light the silver lamps
> Of eve? Why give me eyes to see, and soul
> To love so strong and deep? Then, with a pang
> This brightness stabs me through, and wakes within
> Rebellious voice to cry against all death?
> Why set this hunger for eternity
> To gnaw my heartstrings through, if death ends all?
> If death ends life, then evil must be good,

Wrong must be right, and beauty ugliness.
God is a Judas who betrays his son,
And with a kiss, damns all the world to hell,
If Christ rose not again!

O we must cling to faith in the good God and his goodness!

The Voice of Belief

Death does not have the last word, because belief testifies. Dean Lynn Harold Hough, of Drew Seminary, made this profound statement in one of his sermons: "You can test a civilization by its capacity for tremendous beliefs. The civilization which has become unable to believe in immortality has ceased to deserve immortality." It does matter much what a man believes. It make a difference in his living. There is too much loose talk about the unimportance of a creed. Life must have some creed to live by. That creed will come to expression in what a man is and what he does. If man believes that his final destination is the grave, what is the real worth of struggle and overcoming opposition? If man believes that he is of eternal worth, the worth of struggle and opposition is in discipline and victory. There are eternal results to be had now in our living.

Martineau remarked that we do not believe in immortality because we can prove it, but we try to prove it because we cannot help believing it. The psalmist exclaimed: "I shall be satisfied, when I awake, with thy likeness"! There does not seem to be any other lasting satisfaction. The life of eternity has contentment in it. The spiritual values of life are imperishable. There must be another world to remedy the imperfections of this one. If man reaches out for the highest, there must be the highest for his crowning day. God will bring reality to man's dreams, success to his purpose, and completion to his task. *Immortality is less of a problem when it becomes more of an experience.*

There have been many sincere laborers for world peace, without apparent reward. It looks like death has the last word in war. Yet the big guns have not shelled the Sermon on the Mount. There are those who still believe in Christ as the Prince of Peace and hear him say: "Blessed are the peacemakers: for they shall be called the children of God." Someday peace will come. Meanwhile let Christians abide in the peace of God, and extend good will to others.

The belief in life after death is a tremendous belief. It encourages continued faith in the possible best. For that faith we are willing to live and prepared to die. It makes for patience in suffering. It gives strength for weakness. It lights the skyline of tomorrow. It sets life on the side of right, which will win at the long last.

The Voice of the Past

Death does not have the last word because the past witnesses. The shout of early Christianity is the eternal truth that Jesus Christ our Lord rose from the dead. The story of the Christian Church would end in bitterest tears if it ceased to preach Christ alive forevermore. The power of an endless life in him must be the resurrection power for a world dead in trespasses and sins. The experience of Christian believers

106

across the centuries is that "our Saviour Jesus Christ
. . . . hath abolished death, and hath brought life and
immortality to light through the gospel." To be sure,
there was life before Jesus came into the world; men
held dear the thought of immortality ere his coming.
But his advent made more radiant the blessings of one
and the hope of the other.

Jesus convinced men that he had come from God.

Jesus made men believe that he was going to God.

Jesus, under closest observation and heaviest pressure, witnessed to spiritual reality in his living.

Before he ever wore the crown of thorns he saw
himself the victor over death. Before he was fastened
to the cross he saw the stone rolled away from the
sepulcher. What happened after Jesus died? He arose
triumphant over death and the grave. The church
established its firm position in the light of that historic
fact. Its mind and heart treasured the truth and power
and fellowship of the Resurrection. Upon the rock
of a living faith in their Lord alive the early Christians
stood and challenged the very gates of hell to prevail
against them. *The sin-conquering, death-defying
Saviour lived again!* There was a great boldness to
withstand all the armies of evil.

The Resurrection accounts for despairing disciples'
becoming the evangels of hope.

The Resurrection transformed discouraged followers into the saints of martyrdom.

The Resurrection lit deepest gloom with the fires of
persecution.

The Resurrection broke the seal of empire and doomed the might of the Caesars.

The voice of the past is on the side of the empty tomb. The certainty of Christ's survival, the evidence of reliable witnesses, the authority of the Scriptures, the Sunday of worship, the existence of the church—all testify against death. Death does not have the last word to

> Push eternity from human thought,
> And smother souls immortal
> In the dust.

The Voice of Love

Death does not have the last word because the heart makes its declaration. Wrote George Herbert Palmer of his much-loved wife: "Though no regrets are proper for the manner of her death, who can contemplate the fact of it and not call the world irrational, if out of deference to a few particles of disordered matter it exclude so fair a spirit?" Even the agnostic Ingersoll uttered heart's desire at his brother's grave: "In the night of death hope sees a star, and listening love can hear the rustle of a wing." The psychologist William James affirmed his faith in a memorial address for Francis Boott: "Goodbye, then, old friend, goodbye. We shall never more meet the upright figure, the blue eyes, the hearty laugh, upon these Cambridge streets. But in that wider world of being, of which this little Cambridge world of ours forms so infinitesimal a part, we may be sure that all our spirits and their missions here will continue in some way to be represented, and that ancient human loves will never lose their own." And Tennyson prayed:

> Ah Christ, that it were possible
> For one short hour to see
> The souls we loved, that they might tell us
> What and where they be.

The fourteenth chapter of John is most comforting in its message to sorrowing hearts and lonely lives. On the eve of his departure from his disciples, Jesus talked of the life beyond. He did not go into any details about it. *He did give assurance of it.* He ministered tenderly to troubled hearts, and asked that they be not troubled. He began there a lasting fellowship with his loved ones. An earthly separation would not end their being with him. He left the way open to the Father's House of Many Rooms. He bade them continue in that way.

"Our Saviour Jesus Christ .... hath abolished death, and hath brought life and immortality to light through the gospel." We have not lost forever our loves. We shall meet again. Troubled hearts, lonely folk, look up and carry on! Christ will keep the eternal hope before you and will bring you to himself "beyond the clouds and beyond the tomb."

X

HEAVEN IS REAL

"Joy Cometh in the Morning"

THE NIGHTS of this life are but prophetic of the eternal day to dawn. Clouds and darkness that have shut out the stars here will never drape the sky of Glory. Says the inspired writer of Revelation: *"There shall be no night there."*

When this preacher had talked about heaven in a certain church, an old man, with new light on his wrinkled face, said: "That's the first sermon on heaven I've heard in fifteen years. It did my soul good." Yes, the old man was nearing the end of life's journey. But the others of us may be nearer the end than we think. Our loved ones and our friends are leaving us. We too shall have to go. I believe with the sea-going people of my youth that "we ought to make ready." We should prepare ourselves for the prepared place.

Our subject is not prominent nor popular in the modern pulpit. It is strange that we should insist so upon immortality and eternal life and keep silent about our future abode! If we can wonder at this physical universe which God hath made, why not wonder about his new universe for the redeemed? True it is that we do not know a lot about heaven. True it is also that our knowledge is limited concerning the earth. There is, however, an interest and urgency in mystery. We do not stop living when we fail to understand. One of the most precious of old hymns sings of heaven's morning breaking after earth's darkness deepens. That is not just sentiment foreign to the need of modern man. There are human needs that abide. Humanity will not give up heaven. It is a shining lamp in the darkness. *Heaven's reality is needed now.* No blackout can hide the City of God. Men see it through their tears and die with its hope in their hearts.

Let not life be deceived into thinking that it is unnecessary to preach of heaven. Some of us know differently from that. We have heard the testimonies and prayers of those

> Waiting till over Paradise the sun
> Shall rise in majesty, and life begun
> Shall glow in glory, as the perfect day
> Moves on to hold its endless, deathless sway.

Moreover, some of us have known the lonely places in our own broken homes.

"I Go to Prepare a Place"

The message of the Christian gospel is not the message of "one world at a time." One of the last truths uttered by Jesus was the reality of the hereafter. It was very real to him. Beyond the cross and the tomb he was returning *home.* His redeemed should be there with him.

The evangelists of the church have linked two worlds together in their preaching for souls.

111

John Wesley, scholarly Christian and founder of Methodism, "whose dead hand has rung church bells around the globe," wanted to make sure of reaching heaven.

Great and good living was done when our fathers and mothers used life as a preparation for the other land.

I will not soon forget the statement made by Bishop Hughes when presiding over us for the last time. He moved our conference with his words: "I am on my way to heaven, and I don't intend to get lost!"

O people, it is not a mark of intellectual failure to preach the reality of heaven! Rather is it a needed grip on an eternal truth for the experiences of time. "One must be afflicted with spiritual stupidity or cursed with incurable frivolity who has never thought of that new state on which he may enter at any time, nor speculated concerning its conditions." So declared Ian Maclaren. Neither is the preaching of heaven an outmoded emotional appeal. God pity us when emotion is gone! Religion needs brains to keep it from blowing up, but it needs feelings to keep it from freezing to death.

"*A City Which Hath Foundations*"

Heaven is real as the City of God. From olden time when faithful Abraham went out in search of the City until now with the adventurer of faith, heaven has called man onward. Its permanency has remained through ages of change.

It was a boyhood ambition of mine to see someday

the city of man. It was a worthy dream of the countryside, and it came true. I remember well that first voyage of night up the Chesapeake Bay, and Baltimore on the skyline in the morning. The memory of that trip still thrills. Why should it be dismissed as sentimental nonsense when one thrills at these verses of Holy Writ? "Wherefore God is not ashamed to be called their God: for he hath prepared for them a city." "Eye hath not seen, nor ear heard, neither have entered into the heart of man, the things which God hath prepared for them that love him."

The city of man gets larger. Its skyscrapers cover the opening of sky. Its crowds lose the individual. Its lack of space denies a garden. Its noises drown out the singing of birds. The city of man is suggestive of man's need in his spirit. He wants the sky and human fellowship, the flowers and songs. In the City of God, appropriately named by Fred Shannon "the Land of Room Enough," man will dwell in the perfect city.

There will be a lighted sky: "The glory of God did lighten it, and the Lamb is the light thereof."

There will be sweeter fellowships than earth ever knew: "Behold, the tabernacle of God is with men, and he will dwell with them, and they shall be his people, and God himself shall be with them, and be their God. And God shall wipe away all tears from their eyes."

Life shall have a more beautiful garden: "And he shewed me a pure river of water of life, clear as crystal, proceeding out of the throne of God and of the

Lamb. In the midst of the street of it, and on either side of the river, was there the tree of life, which bare twelve manner of fruits, and yielded her fruit every month: and the leaves of the tree were for the healing of the nations."

Heaven will have earth's redemption set to music: "And they sung as it were a new song before the throne. . . . . And no man could learn that song but the hundred and forty and four thousand, which were redeemed from the earth."

Heaven will be the Holy City: "And there shall in no wise enter into it any thing that defileth, neither whatsoever worketh abomination, or maketh a lie: but they which are written in the Lamb's book of life."

"Sometime We'll Understand"

The separations of life make heaven real. Bishop Simpson cried out during an impassioned deliverance: "What would heaven be without my Willie?"

We need heaven to fill the vacancy of a lonely heart. The feeling runs deep that we shall have out loved ones again, and lose them no more.

> When man's dearest dies, 'tis then he goes
> To that old balm that heals the centuries' woes

The minister recalls the suffering he has seen in his pastorates. The reality of heaven lit the darkness of pained bodies and disturbed minds and downcast spirits. He has heard the lamentations of love, and seen the heavy leaning on God. "There shall be no night there." One of the best and hoped-for blessings of heaven will be God's revelation of his ways with life in trial and tribulation.

"Loved Ones Over Yonder"

Longfellow in his poem "Footsteps of Angels" writes of "the beloved, the true-hearted" coming to visit him once more. Wordsworth puts faith on the lips of a child in "We Are Seven," the child counting the dead as present members of the family. There is a spiritual communion with our remembered dead, and that makes heaven real. Let the church be glad when it recites in the creed: "I believe in . . . . the communion of saints." The good feeling will not down, thank God, that we shall meet our loved ones again.

On the tomb of Bunsen, the chemist, there is inscribed in Latin: "*Amavimus, amamus, amabimus.*" His dying whisper to his wife was: "We have loved, we love now, we shall love forever." Love is stronger than death. Love goes on loving. Jesus wanted his followers to love. His own love could not be conquered. It could speak forgiveness from the cross and open the gates of Paradise to a redeemed thief. So may we love in life's darkest and hardest hour. "There shall be no night there."

We shall know each other in heaven. If the pagans believed in meeting and knowing again, why should the pulpit be hesitant as to reunion and recognition? Why permit people to go to sources outside the church and make inquiries of the hereafter?

Heart, you and I must journey up the years,
And at the top when weary and travel-worn,
Tried with the storm of battle we have borne,
The happy welcome from our little son
Will make but still more sweet the Master's soft "Well done."

"His Servants Shall Serve Him"

Life's unfinished tasks make heaven real. Even God cannot get everything done here. It will require eternity for him to finish that which he has begun in us. There is an incompleteness about the work of man. Beecher was walking through a cemetery with a friend. "Well," said the former, "I suppose they will be bringing me out here before long and leaving me. But God knows I won't stay here." "Where shall we look for you, Mr. Beecher?" queried his friend. "Somewhere, doing business for God," was the ready response.

It was my rare privilege to know personally the celebrated Negro preacher and great soul, "the Lincoln in Ebony," Charles Albert Tindley. In a sermon on heaven he had pictured with his artistry of words Christ as the Light. Then his voice rose in pleasing volume: "I am going to study the mystery of Godliness in the libraries of the sky by this Blessed Light." Man at his best wants an industrious immortality. He conceives heaven as offering further and full opportunity for achievement and service.

It looks as if literature lost Arthur Hallam all too soon. Frederick Robertson, preacher of preachers, died before forty. Raphael was lost to art, Mozart to music, Keats to poetry, all in the earlier and promising years of life. The lesser known have had life's sun to go down while it was yet day. Hear, O my soul! "There shall be no night there." Whatever work there be for hands by and by, the limitations of earth and fact of death will never interfere.

"Going Home"

When O. Henry lay dying, his attendant dimmed the light by the bed. Came the feeble request from the author: "Put on the light. I don't want to go home in the dark." Home makes heaven real. For many the old home of childhood is no more. For others the new home circle is broken. Our people are in heaven's census. It is not uncontrolled emotion when we sing from our hymnal:

> More homelike seems the vast unknown
> Since they have entered there.

If "home is where the heart is," there is some homesickness for heaven in this strange, lonely world.

We too must move on. We come from a far land. We do not live here always. We join the march of those pilgrims of the faith that "desire a better country, that is, an heavenly."

It made news when the columnist Heywood Broun turned to religion. Soon after his passing, Christopher Morley wrote of him: "He always took an innocent pleasure in being what used to be known as a Man about Town; and little by little he discovered that the Town that is most interesting is the City of God."

Interesting? Yes. There is a destiny to match the thought of man. There is a reward for his faith. There is a fulfillment to his hope. There is a reunion in love. There is a crowning for his life. There is eternity for his heart.

Date Due
